Controlling the Debt Monster

A Guide to Managing Your Money

Tessa-Marie Shillingford

authorHOUSE®

AuthorHouse™
1663 Liberty Drive, Suite 200
Bloomington, IN 47403
www.authorhouse.com
Phone: 1-800-839-8640

First published by AuthorHouse   3/12/2009

ISBN: 978-1-4389-6394-5 (sc)
ISBN: 978-1-4389-6393-8 (hc)

Printed in the United States of America
Bloomington, Indiana

This book is printed on acid-free paper.

Table of Contents

Why I Wrote This Book

I remember telling my manager at the financial institution where I work that I was writing a book on financial planning. His reply to me came in the form of a question: "Do you know how many financial planning books there are?" My answer was that I couldn't find one like the one I was writing. "What is so different about yours?"

"Just you wait and see," I said, and walked away.

I knew my book was different. I knew that the people I was aiming to share my knowledge with are people who have never been taught Money Management 101. They are people whose incomes are from $15,000 to $100,000 and they don't know how they are spending their money. I wrote this book for people who would like to be able to save money so that one day they can own a home, go on a vacation, pay for summer camp for their children or for a special occasion.

I also wrote for the many people I have met during my career as a financial advisor who came to me for financial advice and could not tell me their exact income. The answers were generally "about $40,000" or "close to $50,000 annually"; the hourly rates were even more confusing: "$10 and something" or, most commonly, "fifteen and change." It is so important to know exactly how much money you make, and you need to know without flinching. If you do not know how much you make, how can you determine how much you have to spend?

I wrote this book for people who are earning $19,000 and owe $15,000 in credit card debts, and also for those who are paying 19% or more on revolving credit. I wrote it for people who get paid and have no choice as to how their income gets spent. I wrote it for people who want to control their debt, for people who know that what is happening to them financially is not how it is supposed to go, but do not know what to do. And I wrote this book for the self-employed person who needs to understand the basics of small-business banking.

I wrote this book to help you save for fun. Instead of throwing that next vacation onto the credit card, plan for the trip and spend the year saving for it in advance. That way there will be no "buyer's remorse." Your financial institution will help you arrange that—it will take a less than thirty-minute trip to your bank, or you can do it on the Internet.

Everyone needs a safety net. It might take a while, but start saving for three to six months' living expenses. You can have your financial institution do that automatically for you with a money-market mutual fund, but make sure you start. The amount is up to you, but you must start.

Be aware of the cost of carrying a credit-card balance every month. The most expensive debts are department store credit cards. Know your interest rate and make sure you pay off your balance every month. It's better to buy on credit only what you can pay off every month in full.

Be sure to have credit protection — that is, make sure that if you or your spouse were to die you would not leave your family with a load of debt and no credit protection. Be aware of the cost of that unprotected debt for your family.

Finally, I wrote this book so that you'll know exactly what is happening in your financial life. The company you work for knows that; when the forecast is not going their way, they stop, regroup, and make changes. Your finances should not be any different. The company where you work will lay people off, subcontract, close some divisions for a few months, or discontinue a particular product or activity. In other words, it will make some very hard and controversial changes in order to increase its positive bottom line. In your financial life you should do the same: cut back to going only once a month to the movies or out to dinner, bring your own lunch, shop carefully — only buy what you need and can afford.

That's why I wrote this book.

Chapter 1

"We Need Your Help!"

One cold winter evening while I was enjoying a particularly good book, the doorbell startled me. To my surprise it was my sister's daughter Angela and her boyfriend, Lucas.

"Hi, Aunt Tess," she said, and before I could even reply, "we need your help! Mom said that I should come and see you right away. She told me you're a financial advisor who provides advice to people who want to improve their financial situations. She also told me that you've helped a lot of people and that you really know your stuff."

I stood there with my mouth open, clutching my robe, and peered at the young man standing behind her. He seemed less enthusiastic and uncomfortable, as if he did not want to be here.

"Come in, come in." I ushered them into the living room.

The phone started ringing. A few seconds later my husband shouted, "Tessa, grab the phone."

"Take a message," I shouted back.

He came upstairs. "Oh, that's funny, Angela — you're here. Your mother is on the phone." Angela leaned forward to take the phone. "She wants to talk to you, Tess."

"Hello," I said, still clutching my robe.

"Oh, Tessa, don't tell me Angela and Lucas are really at your house."

"Okay, I won't tell you."

"Oh, stop being funny," she snapped. "Tessa, I didn't expect her to jump in the car and head over to your house so late. She was just over here stressing about how she and Lucas are strapped financially and I suggested that she talk to you. I thought she would call and make an appointment to see you at work. Really, Tess, I did not expect her to rush over to your house tonight."

"Well," I said, "she's probably just really worried. How did you know that she was here?"

"Her sister told me that Angela had left and was apparently heading over to your place to see you tonight."

"Well, she's here now, so I'm going to go see what's going on. Don't worry about it. I'll talk to you tomorrow."

"Anyone in the mood for tea?" I looked over at my niece, who looked as if she was rethinking the whole idea of coming over.

"Oh, Aunt Tess, I'm so sorry. We'll leave now and I'll call you tomorrow to book a time that's more convenient for you."

"Oh no," I said, thinking to myself, *This challenge is mine.* I had just been waiting for my cue. I had heard a rumour through the family grapevine that Angela was having some financial problems. If I had jumped in and tried to help, someone would have said, "Here goes Tess, Miss Know-It-All!" I usually just wait until someone comes knocking . . . as Angela did tonight. This opportunity was not going to escape me — I was going to help her!

"So, young lady," I said while putting the kettle on, "I am going to make us some tea and you are going to tell me what's going on."

Thoughts were running through my mind as I made the tea. Dealing with clients is quite a different experience than dealing with the financial troubles of family members. You have to be tough, yet move cautiously. I was very concerned about Angela. I have always had a special place in my heart for her. How deep had they managed to get themselves? I kept picturing my niece, who looked so worried. That's when I had to catch myself. *Just talk to them, Tess,* I told myself. *First just see how bad it really is.*

I brought the tea out to them and said, "Okay, tell Aunt Tess what's going on — "

Before I could finish my sentence Angela started venting. "Aunt Tess, you would not believe the mess we're in! I can't believe it, especially considering all the money we earn!" She spread her hands about thirty centimetres apart.

"That much?" I said.

"Aunt Tess, we have about three times that in bills."

"Oh." I tried not to show my concern as I poured tea and opened a tin of cookies.

"Yes, Aunt Tess, and it is so overwhelming."

"Okay, it's 9 p.m. and you have about a forty-five-minute drive home. You need to rest for work tomorrow. Why don't we enjoy our tea, relax, and make plans to meet on a day and time suitable to all three of us. What about Saturday, around 4 p.m.? Does that work for you?"

"That will be great," Angela replied, with relief in her voice.

I then addressed Lucas. "What about you, Lucas? Does Saturday work for you?"

"You mean I should be there too? Can't Angela handle this?"

I tried to contain myself. "No! Don't you have debts? Aren't you two planning a life together? I am sure you both told me you're planning to get married. If you both have debts, I suggest you work through them before you take any big steps."

"Yes, I know, but—"

"It's important that you both attend the meeting. What about Saturday at 4 p.m.? How does that work for you?"

"Well, I play soccer on Saturdays." Lucas was really trying to avoid the meeting. This is to be expected when people are knee-deep in debt—the mere thought of confronting the details creates an almost unbearable level of anxiety.

"Okay, let's look at another option. I've booked off work on Monday. Let's say Monday at 6 p.m."

They both agreed. They were just about to leave when I told them they had a homework assignment. I handed them a standard form I use to assist clients when they are listing monthly income and expenses. I wrote down the things that I needed them to bring on Monday, a list that included all of their monthly income, expenses, and debts, for example, credit card statements, loan statements, etc. I gave them their list of necessities, handed them their coats, and kissed them goodbye.

As I was getting ready for bed later, my husband asked, "What was that all about?"
"That, honey," I replied, "is my next challenge."

Summary

- Stay calm.
- It's okay to ask for help.
- Every member of the family needs to participate in fighting the Debt Monster.
- Gather and prepare all financial statements (pay stubs, credit card bills, household expense bills, etc.).
- Have a journal ready to record spending.

Reader's Notes

Review your income and expenses. Then write down your thoughts.

_____

_____

_____

_____

_____

_____

_____

_____

_____

_____

_____

_____

_____

_____

_____

_____

_____

_____

Chapter 2

Realization

Angela and Lucas, Week One: Our First Meeting

Monday evening, at exactly 6 p.m., the doorbell rang. When I answered the door, I was surprised to see my niece and Lucas standing in front of me holding what looked like a bag of takeout Chinese food — a large bag. They were both grinning from ear to ear with eagerness.

"Hello, Aunt Tess," they said in unison.

"Come in, come in," I said, smiling.

"Mom suggested that we bring you dinner, so we picked up some Chinese food from our favourite spot on our way over here. I bet you've never had Chinese food like this before. I only hope we brought enough," Angela said, resting the bag on the kitchen counter.

"The food smells heavenly," I smiled. Even though I was pretty hungry I couldn't help being concerned, and I made a mental note to ask my sister to discourage this young lady from buying takeout. Ordering takeout is a habit that many people have fallen prey to. Of course, ordering takeout saves you from having to cook; however, it costs substantially more than a home-cooked meal.

Angela had brought enough food to feed twelve people. She asked where her cousins and my husband were, saying, "I brought enough for everyone."

"They're not home," I answered. "Anyway, we have lots to do, so the three of us will eat and then we can get to work. The others will eat as they come home."

After dinner I asked Lucas and Angela for the list of their income and expenses and the statements of all their debts. Demonstrating their diligence and commitment to the task, they had brought everything I asked for. I handed each of them a new journal.

"Let's begin. First we must establish how much money you earn after tax, because *that* is the amount you have to live on. List your income before and after tax and other employer-related deductions on the first page of each of your journals. On the next page you will need two columns with the headings 'Income' and 'Expenses.' Write down the frequency of your pay — is it weekly or biweekly? This exercise is going to help you to remember all of your expenses. From now on, every month, when you're working on your finances, you'll be able to reference what you have to pay out.

"As a couple living together, you must share some common expenses. Aside from the common expenses, I'm assuming that you must also have separate expenses. List your portion of all the fixed expenses that you share — for example, rent, food, phone, cable, household insurance — and then list all your other personal expenses."

After about fifteen minutes Lucas stopped writing. He just sat there, staring at the page and his stack of bills. When I looked over at Angela, she was running her hands through her hair and sighing. They both looked baffled.

"Guys, what is going on?" They both looked at me with their mouths open.

"Lucas, what's the problem?"

"I'm frightened," he said.

Angela blurted out, "Frightened and confused. I feel lost and so stupid. Aunt Tess, this is hard to swallow. I know that my income isn't enough to support all of these expenses, and let's not forget my other needs."

"Yeah," said Lucas, "something is wrong. There's money left over—uh, there *should* be money left over—but I can't find it."

We were right on schedule. This is the part of the exercise that shocks a lot of people. Seeing it in black and white really drives the message home.

"What do you mean?" I asked.

"Okay, without even adding my bills and living expenses, I should have money left over. According to this breakdown, I don't have it! I don't even have any savings, so it's not hidden. Where is the money I thought I had?" Lucas sounded exasperated.

"That money was probably used for miscellaneous expenses," I said. "Okay, what I want both of you to do is add your expenses and then subtract them from your income. If your income is less, that's okay. I need your figures, regardless of surplus or deficit."

After a few moments of calculating, Lucas stated, "I should have a surplus of $1,200."

"And I need $500 more just to pay all my bills and my living expenses," said Angela. "No wonder I'm in trouble!"

"Well," I said, "this is what I want you to do—"

"More?" wailed Angela. "I'm exhausted!"

"Well, I guess we can call it a night then, but I'm sending you off with more homework. Over the next week I would like you to keep track in your notebook of every penny you spend. That means even when you buy gum or coffee, write it down. I mean every penny."

"How do we do that?" asked Lucas, looking perplexed. This all seemed so foreign to him—something I was about to change.

"If you buy one coffee and one donut on Monday, write it in your journal. If you buy your lunch, write it down. Like I said, even a packet of gum must be entered in your journal. This is called journaling your expenses—everything is to be listed in your notebook." They looked overwhelmed. "By taking the time to account for your spending, you will know where your money is going."

"Well, that's great for Lucas," Angela said desperately. "He's supposed to have money left over. From what we have done so far, I can see I'm just not making it! What's the point of this exercise anyway?"

"The point of this exercise is to help you get a clear picture of where your money is going." I could tell they were becoming discouraged.

"But I *know* where it's going. I'm simply not making enough money."

"This is the exercise I have asked you to do," I said, looking at her with my serious, do-it-because-I'm-your-aunt-and-I-said-you-should face.

"Okay, I'll do it, but I'll tell you this: I'm not enjoying it. I'm nervous! I have a headache now."

"I understand, but please do your homework. I'll see you same time next week."

That concluded our meeting. Looking as if they had the weight of the world on their shoulders, Angela and Lucas left. But I didn't worry too much about them. I knew from past experience that they were just in shock. Most people feel that level of anxiety when they take a look at what's coming in versus what's going out. I knew, once they started tracking their daily expenses in a financial journal, that their eyes would be opened, and then I would really be able to help them.

"So, how did it go?" asked my husband later that evening. "I'm pretty sure I heard a lot of sighing. What was that about?"

"You did?" I replied. "That, my dear, was expenses climbing over income."

Summary

- On the first page of your journal, list your income — before and after tax and employer deductions.
- Create two columns labelled "Income" and "Expenses."
- Write down all fixed expenses, regardless of whether they are separate or shared.

- List all your personal and other expenses.
- Add up all the expenses and subtract then from your income.

Homework: Keep track of all your expenses throughout the week. List every single thing you buy, including that pack of bubble gum.

Reader's Notes

List your feelings about this exercise.

_____

_____

_____

_____

_____

_____

_____

_____

_____

_____

_____

_____

_____

_____

_____

_____

_____

_____

_____

Chapter 3

Facing the Monster the Way It Is

Angela and Lucas, Week Two: Small Expenses

Angela and Lucas came promptly at seven, and this time I could feel their excitement. After our initial greetings they both sat down eagerly and opened their workbooks right away.

Lucas spoke first: "I must say, the last week has been a huge eye-opener. This idea of keeping a journal of my expenses really shocked me. It seemed that the money was leaving my wallet before I could get a chance to document it. Boy, it was really hard to do, but I did it."

Before I could say a word, Angela piped up. "You have no idea how difficult this was to do. I felt like I was having a tug-of-war between my money and myself. I had to grab onto my money and actually say, 'Oh no, you're not leaving my wallet until I write down where you're going.' Aunt Tess, that was hard to do."

"As your grandmother would say," I replied, "take care of the pennies and the dimes will take care of themselves.

From what you've been saying it looks like both of you kept track of how your money was spent. This is one of the most important steps in financial control. On your way to financial independence you need to know how your money is spent, which will enable you to make changes and to keep more of your money.

"Now tell me, Lucas, from the expenses you recorded, where can you make changes to retain some of your money?"

"You remember I couldn't account for a large sum of money from my paycheque? Well, that money came out by debit card and cash. I found out I was spending about $6 every day for a coffee and donut for breakfast. Then I was spending about the same for lunch, and sometimes I would even buy a mid-afternoon chocolate bar. I was spending from $17 to $20 a day on these purchases. I spent that amount every day this past week, and I know I spend this amount about twenty times a month.

"Also, Angela and I go to this gourmet coffee shop on Saturdays and Sundays, and that's about $20 each visit. Then there is the money we spend going out to dinner and a movie every Tuesday. Although Tuesday is discount night at the movies, our dinner isn't discounted, so that's another $40 every week."

"Did you ever give this any thought before? Did you realize you were spending that much money every day?"

"No," replied Lucas. "I swiped my card or spent the cash. On Thursday night when I went home I started mentally doing the math, and I became concerned, then appalled — I could not believe I was spending that much money."

While I was taking in Lucas's remarks, Angela said, "The way I spend you would think I owned the Canadian Mint or that I'm an Automated Banking Machine. I found myself swiping my bank card for a pack of gum. The realization hit me, and I almost choked while entering my PIN. That was how my Friday went. On Sunday morning we decided we would eat at home, and it was during that meal that we started looking at our spending habits over the past week on the small things we purchased."

"Can you tell me what you learned from this exercise?" I asked.

"Okay," said Angela, "from this exercise I found out that I am an impulsive and undisciplined consumer."

"And you, Lucas?"

"I found out that I'm impulsive too," Lucas responded, looking ashamed.

"Have you thought about what you can do to help yourselves? From what you've been saying, I gather you're not happy with what is happening with your money."

Lucas said, "We're both unhappy with our spending habits and we want to cut back, of course."

"That's good," I said, "but I would like to take the exercise a little further and have you both list all the automatic expenses you have coming out of your accounts, such as gym memberships, loan debits, bills, etc. I also want you to continue keeping track of your daily expenses and come up with a plan you think you can live with. I'll advise you on implementing your plan."

Summary

- Find out how your money is spent.
- The little things you buy on a daily basis soon start to add up.
- Realize that there are things you can probably cut back on.

Homework: List all automatic payments coming out of your accounts and think about the changes you want to make.

A Note to the Reader

In this chapter my plan is for you to look at how you spend your money. It is sometimes difficult to put it all down on paper. My role here is to encourage you to make the decision to work with your partner or, if you are single and on your own, to find out exactly what you do with your money. The main thing to remember is that several small amounts—for example, for a daily cup of coffee or some gum—all add up to one large amount. And at the end of a period that amount will have a big impact on your finances. Be sure to work through this exercise a few times and then again to be clear about your spending.

Reader's Notes

What have you learned so far about your spending habits?

_____

_____

_____

_____

_____

_____

_____

_____

_____

_____

_____

_____

_____

_____

_____

_____

_____

_____

_____

Chapter 4

Taming the Monster

Angela and Lucas, Week Three:

1. Recognizing impulsive shopping
2. Monitoring automatic charges from accounts
3. Listing regular expenses

"Good evening, Aunt Tess. How are you?"

"Oh, I'm absolutely wonderful," I said. "And how are you two?"

"We're just great. Lucas and I have been keeping track of our spending as you suggested. We've listed all the automatic payments, both shared and personal, from our accounts, and we've also worked on a plan to cut back on our impulsive spending!"

"That sounds great. It seems that you two had a very productive week."

"Oh yes," said Lucas. "We've spent hours and hours talking and taking notes. We both feel really charged, for the first time in years."

"Can I see what you've done?"

Here are the lists they gave me:

Weekly Impulsive Spending

LUCAS		ANGELA	
Morning			
1 coffee @ $1.20 × 5 days =	$6.00	1 tea @ $1.20 × 5 days =	$6.00
1 bagel @ $1.15 × 5 days =	$5.75	1 bagel @ $1.15 × 5 days =	$5.75
Afternoon			
1 juice @ $1.35 × 5 days =	$6.75	chocolate @ $1.00 × 5 days =	$5.00
gum @ $1.50 × 5 days =	$7.50	1 water @ $1.00 × 5 days =	$5.00
1 water @ $1.00 × 5 days =	$5.00		
Subtotal	**$31.00**	**Subtotal**	**$21.00**
Saturday Morning		Sunday Morning	
Specialty Coffee Shop	$21.75	Specialty Coffee Shop	$21.75
(Lucas pays for Saturdays)		(Angela pays for Sundays)	
Total	**$52.75**	**Total**	**$42.75**
Monthly Total	**$211.00**	**Monthly Total**	**$171.00**

Automatic Payments from Each Account

ANGELA		LUCAS	
Life Insurance	$40.00	Mini-golf membership	$75.00
Gym membership	$49.25	Gym	$47.55
Magazine subscription	$35.75	Business magazine	$33.00
RRSP	$50.00	Cellphone	$40.00
Car insurance	$60.00	House phone	$25.00
Cellphone	$40.00	Car insurance	$125.00
House phone	$25.00	Life insurance	$75.00
Total	**$300.00**	**Total**	**$420.55**

Regular Expenses

ANGELA		LUCAS	
Car payment (new)	$294.00	Rent	$890.00

"This is very good!" I exclaimed. "You've both done very well. Do you have any thoughts about changes you think you should make? That was also part of the homework you had to do."

"Yes, we did," said Lucas, "but we got into a big argument and left it undone."

"That's right," said Angela. "He wanted me to give up my weekly spa treatment, and my magazines, which he said he never sees me read. He's not with me all day, every day, so how does he know what I read?"

"You see what I mean?" said Lucas. "I rest my case." And with that he folded his arms across his chest.

Angela retorted, "Ask him what *he* plans to cut back on. He said he doesn't see where he needs to cut back. I suggested his mini-golf membership. We live in Canada, where it's only warm for a short time, but he pays every month and goes only in July and maybe August."

"Okay, both of you," I said, "time out! Since you couldn't work together to complete this, I'll take you through the exercise myself. Doing this exercise with me means you really have to work at it. Then you will have to do it again before it's finalized." They were both silent.

"Let's look at impulsive purchases. From the list that you provided, your only purchases on a daily basis appear to be small food items such as coffee, etc. Is that an honest picture of what you spend?"

They both nodded.

"So what you're saying is that you never go out to dinner or stop at a fast food restaurant or go to a movie?" This time I wanted them to really think before they answered.

They both looked at me and Lucas said, "The answer is yes . . . we do all of the above." Angela nodded in agreement.

"Well, then, your impulsive buying list is inaccurate. Remember what I said — you need to list every penny you spend. It's only when you know where the pennies go that you can plan ahead and block the pennies' way out."

"We were so proud of what we did," Lucas said, disappointed.

"You should be proud," I replied. "What if you asked any of your friends how much they spend on impulsive purchases? I doubt they would know. Think of what you have accomplished — you should be proud. But as far as the list goes, I need it completed accurately, and please take all the time you need to give me your recommendations for changes."

Summary

- Become aware of all the impulsive purchases you make throughout the week and see how they add up.
- Don't forget to include eating out on your list of impulse purchases.
- Make sure the list is completely accurate — you will only be lying to yourself if you do not include every little purchase on the list.

Reader's Notes

Make your own Weekly Impulsive Spending list:

_____

_____

_____

_____

_____

_____

_____

_____

_____

_____

_____

_____

_____

_____

_____

_____

List the automatic payments that come from each of your accounts:

_____

_____

_____

_____

_____

_____

_____

_____

_____

_____

_____

_____

_____

_____

_____

_____

_____

_____

_____

_____

Now list your regular expenses:

_____

_____

_____

_____

_____

_____

_____

_____

_____

_____

_____

_____

_____

_____

_____

_____

_____

_____

_____

Chapter 5

Automatic Debits

Angela and Lucas, Week Four: Understanding Automatic Debits

"Let's look at your automatic debits."

"We were wondering," said Lucas. "Why do you call them automatic debits?"

"Let me explain. The dictionary defines *debit* as 'a debt that you owe or what you agree to pay.' And *automatic* means the debit comes out on its own electronically, like your life insurance payment. The opposite of debit, which is what I'm hoping you will understand, is called *credit*. The dictionary defines *credit* as 'an amount of money in a bank account, or the opposite of debit.'

"The definition I like most is 'the acknowledgement of achievement—a merit.' What you own and belongs to you *is* an achievement."

"Oh, I understand," said Lucas. "It's the good side of money."

"What do you mean?" asked Angela. "Wait, I get it—I work, and my paycheque is merit for working every day?"

"Yes," I said, "and when you keep most of it you are on your way to being financially sound. I noticed that both of you have life insurance, which I find a bit expensive, considering your ages."

"But our family will benefit immensely if we die. Our friend James just got his life insurance licence and we wanted to show him support—we're trying to help him get started," said Lucas.

"That's very nice," I said. "Your friend James sold you a policy and together you are out $115 every month. I recommend that you let an independent insurance expert take a look at the policy. This is something I will arrange later. Until such time, you both are to continue paying the premiums."

"Why can't you help us with the insurance policy?" asked Angela.

"Insurance, like other special products, should always be discussed with a person trained in that field and licensed to give advice. I am not an insurance specialist.

"I would like you both to look very carefully at your magazine subscriptions, your gym membership, and, Lucas, I really would like you to look at your mini-golf membership. I'm not asking that you cancel all of them, but I would like you to consider some things.

"See if your gym will give you a discount or combine your single memberships. I'm sure there are special rates for couples or families. This might save you 10 or 20 percent. You never know, you may even save as much as 40 percent off the single membership price. You should find out if you can combine your magazine subscriptions also. In some cases a single company owns many different magazines. You may find out that the magazines you both like are owned by the same company and may be able to negotiate a discounted price for your subscriptions.

"Lucas, your golf membership — for what you are paying? Do you really use it? That's something to think about, especially since you spend so much time with Angela now. What you should find out is whether you can include your fiancée for a nominal cost. Make a trip and talk to someone in the office."

"But I thought you were doing all this to help us cut back," said Angela.

"Sometimes, Angela, a small increase in commitment is worth more emotionally than the actual cost. My reason for asking Lucas to do this is to enable him to go to his golf club and to use his membership to spend time with you."

"I understand," said Angela. "And I think I like the idea. My mom would say it's killing two birds with one stone. I'm with him and he's also playing golf."

"I see you're getting it. This is all that I would like you to look after from your automatic debits for this week. Let's recap what you need to work on:

1. Keep a more detailed list of all your expenses, including non-food purchases such as the hockey pool or lottery pool.

2. Check out your gym membership and find out the price for two people from the same family.

3. Combine your magazine subscriptions.

4. Add your fiancée to your golf membership.

"Also, next week we'll be spending a lot of our discussion time on your regular expenses. Take a good look at the area of personal hygiene and grooming, and especially at your credit card purchases. I would like you to bring your most recent credit card statements; if they are not available, phone the company and get the balance owing and the rate of interest you pay on each card. Please make a special effort to have them with you for our next meeting — Monday evening."

Summary

- Automatic debit: a debt that is owed or that you agree to pay that is taken out of your bank account electronically at regular intervals.
- A credit is acknowledgement of achievement — a merit. What you own and belongs to you is an achievement.
- Look over your expenses and see if you can achieve additional savings by combining individual subscriptions or memberships. You may need to get rid of things that are not necessary.
-

Homework: Gather together your most recent credit card statements, along with the interest rates they are charging you. Take a good look at personal hygiene and grooming expenses. Use the next few pages of your journal to keep a detailed list of all your expenses, including non-food purchases. Look at your memberships and magazine subscriptions to check if hidden savings are to be had by combining them.

Tessa-Marie Shillingford

Reader's Notes

_____

_____

_____

_____

_____

_____

_____

_____

_____

_____

_____

_____

_____

_____

_____

_____

_____

_____

_____

_____

Chapter 6

Learning How the Monster Feeds

Angela and Lucas, Week Five: Working Together to Control the Monster

They arrived right on time.

"Hello, Angela, Lucas. I must say I admire the promptness of the two of you."

"We're intrigued by how much needs to be done to tame the monster called 'Spending.' It seems to be crying, 'Feed me, feed me!'"

"Well, let's see if we can find out why the monster has moved in with you guys. Let's talk about your homework. Lucas, you go first."

"This week I documented every time I spent money and I went to my bank's website and checked my account activity every day. This has become a routine. I've kept to purchasing a coffee and donut on Friday mornings only, and I made my lunch every day. I hadn't seen the lunchroom before—I was so surprised to see that even the manager of my department brings his lunch. I was also amazed at how many people brought their lunch, and many of them were executives."

"Purchasing lunch every day is an expensive habit," I said.

"So this week," Lucas continued, "I bought one bottle of water and refilled it at our office drinking fountain instead of buying another one. Also, Angela and I decided to go to the movies and dinner only twice a month instead of four times a month. Oh, by the way, while I was monitoring my account I noticed that my service charges are running up to $30 a month."

"I suggest you go to your bank and discuss your service charges with a representative to see if you have the right account plan," I said. "What else?"

"We're still working on a solution for our weekend visits to the specialty coffee shop."

"Some of the changes you've made are drastic. I suggest that you follow your new plan for a few weeks before making any more adjustments."

"I'm making the same changes as Lucas," Angela said. "Mom was so surprised when I started making my lunches! She's helping me keep on track—she even gives me ideas for what to pack for lunch.

"Both Lucas and I called our magazine companies and found out that although the names are different, they belong to the same company. They have changed our plans to one with one mailing address and that saved us $20.

"We also went to the gym and spoke to a representative. He called us back to say that since we're planning to be married, when our membership expires in two months they'll switch us to a family plan. We'll end up paying full price for one membership and half-price for the other. Then Lucas's manager told him about a fitness place that has a special deal for his company employees, so we're meeting with them tomorrow to see what their discounts are.

"Also, our cellphone company has a special rate for couples. We'll be calling them on Thursday to request a combined plan, which we're hoping will decrease our bill. Lucas also called his home phone carrier, and some of the features on his phone that he doesn't even use are costing him $20 more a month."

"On my cable package I gave up some channels and saved $15," Lucas added, "and I called my mini-golf club. We have an appointment for next Saturday to discuss adding Angela to my membership and what the cost will be."

"So you two have been working hard on the things I asked you to do. What about your regular expenses?"

"We were looking at our clothing expenses and we couldn't see how to decrease that amount. One reason is because we're not sure how or what we actually spend on clothing."

"I was a little curious about that," I said, "because I noticed you did not include expenses for personal hygiene or dry cleaning. What I would like to see you do is keep the amount you've allocated to clothing expenses and then keep track of what you actually spend on clothing, personal hygiene, and dry cleaning in one month. We'll work on aligning that area.

"Now we've come to the most important part of financial control of the 'Debt Monster.' The more debt you accumulate, the more you feed the monster and the stronger it gets."

"I have four credit cards and each card has an interest rate of 18 to 28 percent. My total amount owing is $15,000, on which I pay $600 a month, and the minimum payment varies from $200 to $700 a month." Angela sounded hopeless. "The amount owing never goes down. I looked over my bills for the past three months and the difference from what I owed three months ago is only $6 less. When will I ever pay this thing off?"

"Remember my computer?" Lucas said. "I went to a big-name electronics store and bought my computer on credit. I thought I was buying through the store, but it turned out to be a finance company, and now I pay 32 percent interest. I was so embarrassed at having to use credit that I didn't ask any questions. And I made the same mistake when I bought my furniture—the interest rate is 28 percent. Those two bills never seem to go down. In one year I've decreased my balance by only $98."

"That's the monster—and now you're seeing how it works," I said.

"I owe $15,000 in credit card and financing debt. And that doesn't even include my car. My payments are $900 a month and going nowhere! I feel so angry. If only I'd known what I know now, I would never have found myself in this mess."

"All is not lost," I said. "Next week we're going to look for ways to put the monster on a diet! Meanwhile, just remember your tasks for this week."

Summary

- Find ways to cut down expenses.
- Do not be afraid to ask companies about discounts they might offer — they will not tell you about them unless you ask.
- Minor reductions in your everyday spending will add up to huge savings.
- Every time you accumulate more debt, you feed the Monster and it gets stronger.
- Putting your purchases on a credit card may seem like a good idea at the time, but with the high interest rates these companies are charging, it will seem like forever before you have paid down a fraction of your balance.

Homework: Keep track of what you actually spend on clothing, personal hygiene, and dry cleaning in one month, using the chart provided. Write down your observations and experiences that result from this exercise.

Reader's Notes

Day	Clothing	Personal Hygiene	Dry Cleaning	Laundry (if you pay)
Monday				
Tuesday				
Wednesday				
Thursday				
Friday				
Saturday				
Sunday				

List your observations and experiences from this exercise:

_____

_____

_____

_____

_____

_____

_____

_____

_____

_____

_____

_____

_____

_____

_____

_____

_____

_____

_____

_____

Chapter 7

Finding the Monster's New Menu

Angela and Lucas, Week Six: Deciding How Much to Spend

"Hello, smiling faces!"

"We're really excited," said Angela.

"Great," I replied. "Tonight we are going to put the monster on a slimming diet. From today it will eat only the amount we decide to feed it, and no more. Putting it on this new streamlined diet will really make a difference to its appearance."

"What's the plan?" Lucas asked.

"To control how much and how often the monster feeds, and that depends entirely on you two. I would like you both to visit your banks and speak with someone about your plans and how your bank can help you meet your financial goals. My role here is to prepare you to bank. What I mean by that is to find ways to make your bank work for you and to make you a profitable client—profitable both for you and the bank."

"Make us profitable?" exclaimed Angela. "I can't see it, Aunt Tess. Look at these credit card charges! Now I believe it when they tell us the banks want to keep us poor."

"I understand what you mean," I said. "But you must remember that, although the bank gives you the credit card, you are the ones who decide to use it. Only you can decide to control the habit, and I believe the first thing you need to know is how to control your mindset.

"Remember, each decision you make today determines the life you live tomorrow. When you make a charge purchase today, it affects your cash flow for many months or even longer. What I mean is, learn to say no to more credit. Say, 'No, I don't need another credit card' when it's offered to you. I realize, of course, that you would expect the bank to pay attention to how many cards you're offered and to be generous enough to cut back on your cards and interest rate. But the bank is a business, with shareholders who expect the people who run it to make a profit for them on their investments.

"The two of you are the shareholders in a new company: the Angela/Lucas partnership. The time you invest in running your finances like a company will provide you with a secure financial future. You must choose to manage your finances like a business — to make a profit. You must retain as much as possible from your paycheque by minimizing expenses. This is how one saves money — reduce the monster's diet."

"How do we do this?" asked Lucas. "I am really fired up. I want to keep my money!"

"To keep your money you need to decide some things. First, you must make a decision to get rid of your credit cards — except one. Then you will need to learn to use credit

44

only for what you are able to pay off in full every month. Try to avoid carrying a balance over to the next month, because that balance will just be added to the next month and the next month's balance will be carried over, etc., etc. That balance, along with the interest, is what feeds the monster.

"There are two ways you can pay off these cards. You can increase your payments on the higher-interest cards and work to pay them off, or you can apply for a consolidated loan at your bank."

"Well," said Lucas, "how do we do the second option?"

"Applying for a consolidated loan is a simple process. But I would prefer to know that you've discussed together the decision to apply. So that's it for tonight. But I will end this session by asking you two to do the following:

1. Do some comparison shopping of rates for consolidation loans at the websites of three to four major financial institutions.

2. Do the calculations: look at the various amortization periods (the length of time it takes to pay off the loan), the amount required each month and the interest rates.

3. Discuss whether you should combine your debts and ask for one loan or apply for two separate loans.

"This next exercise I want to be done together:

4. Check your bank's calculations, using the existing balances on your credit cards and the amount you have been paying each month, to see how long it would take you to pay off your debt.

"Next week, bring all this information with you. Remember, this is research. All you are doing is finding out ways to decrease the monster's appetite so that it will be eating less of your after-tax money. We'll meet again same time next week. Have a lovely financially managed week!"

Summary

- Determine when and how much you would like to feed the Debt Monster.
- Banks will continue to give you credit cards, but in the end you are the one who decides to use them, and only you can decide to control the habit. Each decision you make today will determine the life you live tomorrow.
- Put the Debt Monster on a diet by retaining as much as possible from your paycheque and minimizing expenses.
- Reduce the number of credit cards you possess to only one. Be firm in your decision to say no to credit that is offered to you.
- Determine to pay off the high-interest-rate credit cards first or to consolidate all your debts into one loan at your bank.

Homework: Compare rates for consolidation loans at various financial institutions and work out calculations for your debt by looking at the amortization periods, the amount required each month, and the interest rates. Calculate how long it will take to pay off your existing debt with the amount you have been paying each month.

Reader's Notes

_____

_____

_____

_____

_____

_____

_____

_____

_____

_____

_____

_____

_____

_____

_____

_____

_____

_____

Discuss whether you will combine your debts with your partner's and ask for one loan or keep your debts separate and ask for separate loans.

_____

_____

_____

_____

_____

_____

_____

_____

_____

_____

_____

_____

_____

_____

_____

_____

_____

If you are a couple sharing finances, this next exercise should be done together:

Check your bank's calculations, using the existing balances on your credit cards and the amount you have been paying each month, to see how long it would take you to pay off your debt.

_____

_____

_____

_____

_____

_____

_____

_____

_____

_____

_____

_____

_____

_____

_____

_____

_____

_____

Chapter 8

Decisions about the Monster's Menu

Angela and Lucas, Week Seven: Making Some Financial Changes

"Hello, Aunt Tess!" Lucas belted out, with a big grin on his face like someone who had just seen the light.

Angela seemed just as happy. "You know, Aunt Tess, I really look forward to these sessions."

"Oh yes." said Lucas, "We love it!"

"We've learned so much. Do you know Lucas talks to everyone about what we're doing?"

"Yes," said Lucas. "In fact, my friend Peter wants to talk to you."

"Great," I said. "My mission is to enlighten, educate, and encourage everyone I meet to successfully handle their finances."

"That's powerful," said Lucas.

"That's my mission statement," I replied.

"So far, Aunt Tess, you're surely living up to it."

"Thanks," I said. "I'll make time for your friend Peter, but first let's get you two going on choosing which diet the monster will be on."

"Working together on one computer was so difficult at first," Angela said. "We couldn't even decide which website we should go on first. Then we both looked at each other and said, 'You know, let's cooperate — it's our financial future.' Then we relaxed and worked as a team."

"That means my first step for both of you is now in place — working as a team. What did you find out?"

"We found out that the websites for those financial institutions are amazing," said Lucas. "There's so much information. And we found out that borrowing rates are basically the same from one financial institution to another."

"How did you find that out?"

"Well, we compared all the information by printing them out and posting them here on our sheet."

"That's very true," I said. "It was something I needed you to observe."

"How does one make a decision?" asked Angela. "I heard on the radio that you can ask your bank for a better rate."

"Yes, you can," I said, "but you have to evaluate yourself. In other words, when you go to your bank you need to be prepared. In order to negotiate rates, you must have a plan in place. For example, know the rates of the other institutions, speak sensibly, ask questions, and, if you get lost, ask the person who's talking to you to explain what they have just said, especially if they're using bank terminology. One of the things I look for above all else is a bank employee who listens to me and expresses empathy, shows concern, and asks questions, and then makes recommendations."

"That's a lot to digest," said Lucas.

"I know," I answered. "I personally have always looked for eye contact and a genuine smile — and everything else just falls into place. A person who does that is usually ready to help you. Once when I went to a financial institution to deal with my own finances, because of the way the person spoke and his manner I excused myself by telling him I had another appointment elsewhere."

"You certainly are very serious when it comes to what you expect as a customer," said Lucas.

"You see, Lucas, the only thing that separates one financial institution from another is their level of customer service. How does this company treat me? Do I feel my needs are being met? Do they have a willingness to assist me? Do they offer me unique services compared to other places?"

"I feel I can make a better choice after hearing what you just said. I realize that, after looking at the various rates of financial institutions, the only other thing that can help me choose where to go is the level of customer service," said Lucas.

"Great, Lucas," said Angela. "I agree with you — I want us to base our decision solely on customer service, since we've observed that the rates are basically the same."

"Keeping that in mind, what are you going to do about the loan?" I asked.

"We decided go with a consolidation loan for thirty or thirty-six months. Those loans are completely open, so they can be paid off at any time."

"Well," I said, "good work!"

"That's the information we found on the various websites," said Angela. "And we're going to combine our debts, since the interest rate we pay on the amount will be less."

"Good observation." I was so proud of them.

"As you know, we're engaged to be married in three years, and this will enable us to be in a much better financial situation when we do get married."

"It seems that the two of you have really invested a lot of time on your homework. Now, the task I'm giving you for this week's homework is to pay a visit to a bank and make an appointment to get a consolidated loan. I recommend that you visit banks around where you work and check out the level of customer service. Discuss it later and compare your observations, then choose the bank. Make an appointment and, when you do, let them know it's for a loan.

"These are things you will need to take with you for the appointment: a recent pay stub, to let the bank know where you work and how much you make, and the most recent statements for all your credit cards and loans. If you don't have the most recent statement, phone the company and get the balance owing as of today. And you will want to open a joint chequing account for the loan payments to come out of."

"Can we be declined for this loan?" Lucas asked.

"Yes, you can," I answered. "If your credit is bad you can be declined."

"What makes credit bad?" asked Lucas.

"Usually the things that work against you are late payments or no payments, and trying for more credit."

"How do banks find that out?"

"They get this information from credit reporting agencies. Credit card companies and banks report to them on how well you are paying off your credit cards or loans. That information is accessible to all other credit-granting companies. So when you apply for a loan, the company sends a request for your credit report. That report tells the bank how well you have honoured your previous agreements with the companies you owe money to. Every time you ask for credit, the very fine print—usually found at the bottom of the form you've just signed—says a credit check will be done. Even if you are declined, it still gets counted as a time you sought credit."

"This credit and financial stuff sure is complicated and involved. There's so much to getting a loan," said Angela.

"Well, it's getting late, Aunt Tess. We've stayed long enough tonight and my head is full of information to sort out. We love you. See you next week."

"Oh, Lucas, give your friend Peter my number and tell him to call me."

Summary

- Rates are similar from one financial institution to another—it's the level of customer service that separates them from each other. Find a place that provides you with the customer service that you are looking for.
- Come to the financial institution prepared, with your research, when it comes time to negotiating a rate.

- When you have an appointment with a financial specialist, come prepared with a pay stub and the most recent statements for all your credit cards and loans.
- Bad credit usually occurs when you have missed your payments or have sought credit repeatedly.
- All credit-granting companies can access your information from the credit reporting agencies.
- Even if an application is declined, the credit check is still counted because credit was sought.

Homework: Write down the financial changes you want to see happen. Stay focused on your goals and do not get discouraged, even though so many things are changing in your financial life right now. Choose your financial institution carefully and make sure you feel that they want to help you attain your complete financial goal. You are the customer, and customer service is very important in choosing your financial institution.

Reader's Notes

_____

_____

_____

_____

_____

_____

_____

_____

_____

_____

_____

_____

_____

_____

_____

_____

_____

_____

_____

_____

Chapter 9

Peter

Peter, Week One: An Unusual Problem

On Tuesday evening I received a call from Lucas's friend Peter. He sounded very excited and mentioned that Lucas felt I would be able to help him solve his financial problem. I made arrangements to meet with Peter on Thursday evening.

Peter arrived promptly at 7 p.m. He was very nicely dressed and had a warm, firm handshake. After the usual chitchat, I asked Peter to tell me how I could help him financially. He told me he came from a family who believe that if you borrow or use credit cards it means you're not able to make it — and you're considered a failure.

"I've come across this before," I said. "It really is an old way of thinking. It does have its merits, but it also means that no one will ever know whether you have the discipline to honour your commitments and pay your bills on time when you do borrow. That thinking means you buy only with cash, and therefore you buy only what you can afford and when you can afford it."

"Yes," said Peter. "My parents saved for years to buy their house, and they have never borrowed from anyone. The reason I'm here, you see, is because I've always followed my parents' way. When I was at university with Lucas, I was offered a credit card and didn't take it. I am honestly afraid of owning one because of the fear of not being able to pay it back. Then, about two weeks ago, I needed to rent a car — and I couldn't. I had the cash to leave on deposit, but the car rental company needed a credit card. Because of that experience I've been grappling with the idea of applying for credit. I spoke to Lucas about it, and he suggested that I come to see you."

"That was good thinking on Lucas's part," I said.

"The way Lucas speaks of you, one would think you had wings and came from heaven."

I smiled. "There's information you need to know that will enable you to get a credit card, and I'll be glad to guide you through and help. But I will need to ask you some personal and financial questions. Is that all right with you?"

"Sure," said Peter, "I'm here for your help and advice. I'll tell you whatever you need to know."

"How old are you?" I asked.

"Twenty-seven, same age as Lucas."

"Are you employed?"

"Yes, with a management company, for three years now."

"What is your position with company?"

"I'm the manager of our IT department. I was trained as a software designer. Actually, I was the developer of our software."

"You have a very interesting position. Now I have another personal question: are you married?"

"No, not yet." Peter smiled. "I'm presently dating this young lady I met through Angela and Lucas. They're always trying to set me up, and this time they introduced me to a real winner."

"Lovely," I exclaimed. "Now, tell me, Peter, what is your annual income?"

"It's $77,500," he replied.

"Does that include bonuses?"

"No, that's just salary. If my department meets or exceeds our goals, we receive between 10 and 15 percent of our annual income as bonus."

"What savings do you have, Peter?"

"Very little, actually. The person who does my income taxes suggested that I open an RRSP—a registered retirement savings plan—because I always pay additional tax at tax time."

"Why haven't you followed that advice?" I asked.

"My parents don't believe in retirement savings plans. They said they're paying too much income tax and they're very angry. I really don't want this to happen to me."

"During our meetings I'll discuss registered retirement plans and their benefits. While I can provide you with some information to get started, I recommend that you do a little more research regarding RRSPs. The federal government's Internet site will give you all the information you need to make an educated decision. The website for the Canada Revenue Agency is http://www.cra-arc.gc.ca.

"Now let's talk about your credit cards — or lack of them. Peter, to get a credit card you'll need to present a pretty picture of yourself, since you don't have a credit history and, as you mentioned, your savings are very minimal. We need to take some steps to paint a picture that your bank will look at and see your potential."

"Why do I need that?" he asked.

"You see, Peter, your bank doesn't know you. All they can see is your past behaviour, and, as the saying goes, the best prediction of a person's future behaviour is their past behaviour. You have very little in the way of savings. Your bank will look at your financial profile and think, *If he doesn't have the discipline to save regularly, how do we know he will have the discipline to honour the commitment to make payments on his credit card?*"

"I understand," said Peter. "What can I do to let my bank know I'm a reliable person who will stick to his agreement?"

"This is what we're going to work on," I said. "First let me explain what I mean by presenting a lovely, well-balanced financial picture. Let's say you go to an art gallery for the first time and you're standing in front of a canvas that's completely blank. Just a bit farther down the wall is a painting of a small house with trees and a pretty garden, and a big yellow sun in the blue sky overhead. Which one would you look at and feel good about?"

"For me," said Peter, "I would prefer the one with the sky and all those other things."

"That's what I mean. You see, at this moment your financial picture is like an empty canvas. It doesn't portray anything or tell anyone where Peter is headed. You could say that the house represents your savings, the sun represents your job, the garden represents your RRSP, and the trees represent growth, showing that you are constantly saving. The people at a financial institution will see potential. They'll see someone they would want to give a credit card to, because one day you'll come back for a car and a mortgage — and they want you as a customer."

"I've never thought of finances that way," said Peter. "As a matter of fact, I've just never thought of it at all."

"Peter, remember this — what you tend to, grows! Now, I need you to do a few things for me. We're going to meet again next week."

"We are?" asked Peter. "How much do I pay you? This is taking up lots of your time."

"Peter, my pay for helping you, Angela, and Lucas will be knowing I was able to help you develop proper financial habits. I'm fortunate to be blessed with this gift. So what I want from you is, when you've learned all you need to know, teach someone else. How does that sound?"

"You've got a deal," said Peter. "Tell me what you want me to do."

"Next Thursday I want you to bring some information with you:

- the total amount you save and have already saved
- your net pay each payday
- your total expenses, for example, bills, cellphone, and how much you spend on groceries.

"And Peter, bring a calculator and a workbook with pen and pencils."

"Thanks," said Peter. "See you next Thursday, same time."

Summary

- No credit is not the same as good credit. Not having any sort of credit makes it difficult to judge how strong your commitment to payments will be. Something as simple as renting a car will become difficult or even impossible if you do not have a credit card.
- You need to paint a picture for your bank so that it will see your potential. As the saying goes, the best prediction of a person's future behaviour is their past behaviour.

Homework: Peter's situation is very uncommon today, but there are still pockets in the community that continue to deal in cash and only cash. Ever so often these individuals come across that wall of plastic and they have to make the choice to get a credit card — only after they have come across some situation where they cannot do what they want with all the cash in the world. You do need a credit card, but you must be able to control how you use it. If your situation sounds like Peter's, with no credit history, do the homework that Peter was assigned to work on for the week.

Reader's Notes

_____

_____

_____

_____

_____

_____

_____

_____

_____

_____

_____

_____

_____

_____

_____

_____

_____

_____

_____

Chapter 10

Understanding the Bank

Angela and Lucas, Week Eight: How Banks Work—Perception and Appearance

"Hello, Aunt Tess. What an experience! Some banks have no idea what customer service means," exclaimed Lucas. "At this one financial institution, I'd just come from the gym, so I arrived in my sweats. When I approached the front desk, I tried greeting the receptionist with a smile, but she just looked down her nose at me and said, '*Yes?*' I felt like I was back in grade 5, when I stuck some gum in Peter's hair and was sent to the principal's office. My smile just vanished, and I didn't know what to say. So I mumbled something about loans and she told me I needed an appointment.

"Then I remembered what you said about the first person you meet at a financial institution. I looked at the receptionist and said, 'I know I'm in the wrong place,' and then I said goodbye and left. On my way home I was in shock. I just kept thinking, *I need to do this. I'll have to try another financial institution.*"

"Well, I had a much different experience," Angela said. "I went to the bank at lunchtime. When I approached the reception area, a young man greeted me and said, 'How can I help you today?' with a big smile. I explained that my fiancé and I wished to take out a consolidated loan. Then he said he could certainly help me with that, and he would be happy to book me an appointment with one of their financial services representatives. He asked me what time best suited me, and we made an appointment with a lady named Marva for 6 p.m. on Friday. The greeter introduced himself as Paul and gave me a list of things he recommended we bring with us to the appointment. The list was exactly what you told us to bring."

"Obviously, after my experience," said Lucas, "we decided to keep the appointment Angela made.

"We arrived at the bank at 5:45 p.m. and we were greeted by Paul, who told us to have a seat and that he would let Marva know we had arrived. Marva came out to greet us and let us know that she wouldn't be much longer. Five minutes later she asked us into her office. We told her we were early and could wait, but she said she was ready.

"Marva asked, 'How can I be of help to you today?' We told her about our plan for a consolidated loan to pay off our credit cards. We also told her we're trying to put our financial life in order and that we're working with a financial planner. She told us how fortunate we were, and we agreed. Marva asked if we bank with her company and we told her yes, and explained how my pay goes directly into an account at that branch. She explained that would make things easier and asked how much we needed, so we showed her all our credit card statements. We told her we wanted to know whether we would qualify and the payment amount, and then we would take it to you to look over before coming back to sign the forms. She agreed to that and proceeded with the application.

"So here are the papers she gave us. It took almost half an hour to input all the information into the computer. Then she told us she would submit the application to her approval centre, and if everything was in order she would have an answer for us in thirty to forty-five seconds. It came back approved, so here are the documents."

"I see she gave you an application."

"Yes, and during the application process she asked us a few very important questions, such as when we wanted to start paying the loan back and for how long and what our budget for repayment was," said Angela. "But before those questions, she asked us where we worked, how long we had been working for the company, and how much income we earned. I remember she also asked how long we'd been at our present address."

"I really felt bad when she asked if I had any savings," said Lucas. "This was the first time I realized that since I graduated from university I haven't anything to show for four years of being employed."

"I didn't feel quite so bad," said Angela, "because a few years ago I heard you talking to Mom and Dad about RRSPs. You said that instead of Mom and Dad complaining about the amount of taxes they pay, they should take advantage of the legal financial opportunity the government was giving them to save on their income tax. So the very next day I went to the bank and opened an RRSP. I put in $50 each and every payday, and I felt proud to be able to say I had some savings. I have a grand total of $5,750."

"How did you feel when Marva asked you all those questions?" I queried.

"You know," said Lucas, "she did it in such a nice way. She turned her computer screen so we could see it and she leaned towards us to explain why she needed to ask the questions. After each question was answered she asked for our permission to proceed with the next step. That made us feel like we were part of the process."

"Marva sounds like a very considerate person," I said.

"She suggested we try to pay the loan off in thirty months instead of the usual thirty-six. And she gave us two sets of comparison notes that showed we would save money on the interest charges."

"That's a great idea," I said "Thirty months is good. Now what we need to do is list all of your expenses, including the new loan payment. Have you agreed to go for thirty months instead of thirty-six?"

"Oh yes," replied Angela. "We want to have this paid off as soon as possible."

"There's one thing I recommend that you do the next time you see Marva, and that's to open a joint chequing account to handle payment of the loan."

"Hmm, I never thought of where the payment would come from," said Angela.

"That would be the best way," said Lucas. "But which one of us would have the funds to deposit in this new account?"

"This is where automation comes into play," I said. "When you see Marva, have her arrange to have one-third of the payment come from Angela's account into the new account and two-thirds from Lucas's account."

"Why one-third for Angela and two-thirds for me?" asked Lucas.

"It's because your credit cards total twice as much as Angela's," I replied. "Another thing I noticed was that you put in for life and disability insurance on the loan. Was that discussed, and do you understand the insurance?"

"Marva explained that if we were injured and couldn't work, the disability insurance would make the payments, and if one of us died, the life insurance would pay the loan off."

"How did that sound to you?" I asked.

"At first we were hesitant, but then she explained that since we're so young, the insurance amount is very small. And we don't have any other disability insurance, so we agreed to take the loan with both life and disability insurance."

"How did that feel to you?"

"We gave it some thought and decided it was the best."

"I am really glad that you made those choices. Marva can open the joint chequing account when you go in to sign the loan agreement. Ask her to arrange for your separate portions of the loan payment to be transferred at a certain date from your personal accounts to the joint account. I recommend that she does the transfer each payday, so in Angela's case it's half of one-third biweekly and in Lucas's case it's half of two-thirds biweekly from your accounts to the joint account. Your loan payments take effect thirty days after the loan is funded, so if the payments get transferred biweekly, large amounts will never be taken out of your account at one time, thus allowing you always to have money in your single accounts.

"Your homework, my dears, is to each prepare a revised financial plan that includes the one loan payment. That's all for tonight. See you next week," I said. "Goodnight."

Summary

Make sure you find a bank that is ready and willing to help you and your financial needs.

Homework: When you visit the different financial institutions, see how your experiences make you feel. Take notes on how you felt and evaluate how pleased you were with your initial interaction at the bank.

Reader's Notes

Describe your banking experience(s):

_____

_____

_____

_____

_____

_____

_____

_____

_____

_____

_____

_____

_____

_____

_____

_____

_____

_____

Chapter 11

Examining Peter's Finances

Peter, Week Two: Financial Comprehension

Peter arrived early but I could see he was ready to go. He had brought everything I asked him to bring, so we got right into it.

PETER'S INCOME		EXPENSES	
Income biweekly	$1,726	Student loan	$360
Cash kept at home	16,600	Cellphone	60
Chequing account	275	Cable	131
Total	**$16,875**	Lunch	?
		Barber	?
		Hygiene	?
		Clothes	?
		Shoes	?
		Eating out	?
		Movies	?
		Total	$551

"This is it," said Peter. "What's left, I save at home, and I spend what I need when I need to. I live at home with my parents, so I don't pay rent or buy groceries. My parents only want to know that I have some money saved."

"Great," I said, "but, Peter, your financial picture isn't visible to the bank. They know you work, and your paycheque goes to the bank, but you don't keep anything in your chequing account and you don't have a savings account."

"Well, my parents believe that if you keep your money in the bank, the bank pays you interest and then the government makes you pay tax on that interest."

"That's true," I answered, "but then your bank can also give you credit. You see, Peter, your financial picture has no tree, sun, garden, or house. Your bank doesn't know that you have savings at home. I'm recommending that you take the money to your bank, but you will need to explain why you had so much money at your house and not in the bank. I recommend that you phone the bank and ask to see a senior officer. Tell them that you're working with a financial planner and explain your family history with regard to savings. They'll probably make an exception about depositing such a large amount of cash at one time into your account."

"Why is that necessary?" asked Peter.

"The banks are working with the federal government to combat money laundering from crimes such as drug trafficking. Your bank needs to be sure that you're not depositing cash from the sale of drugs or other illegal activities. Money laundering means taking money from drugs or other crime sources and making it legitimate. Passing it through a legitimate account, then taking it out again and depositing it into another account can make it 'clean.'"

"My money isn't drug money!" protested Peter.

"You know that," I said, "but does your bank know that?"

"I see what you mean. Should I ask to see an investment person?"

"First let's get the money to the bank, and then we'll go from there."

Peter looked downcast when he left. "I can't believe the bank might think my money came from organized crime."

"Don't worry," I said. "Your bank will recognize that your family history got in the way. Goodnight, Peter."

Summary

- If you do not keep your money in the bank, they will not be able to see your entire financial picture.
- Remember, the bank can give you credit, but only when they can see the details of your financial picture.

Reader's Notes

Chapter 12

Banks Are for More Than

Cashing Cheques

Peter, Week Three: Tackling the Bank

"Hello, Peter, how are you?"

"Well," he said, "I'm quite pleased. I went to the local branch of my bank and—because of what you told me—I decided to take my parents to the bank with me. I used the terms you suggested and asked for an investment specialist. At first I was told I needed an appointment, but then there was a cancellation and I was able to meet with a specialist named Anne. I explained that I had more than $16,000 in cash. She looked surprised, but my parents being there made it somehow more legitimate—they explained how they felt about banks. Anne then said she needed to speak with the branch manager about my large cash deposit.

"The manager came in and she questioned both me and my parents. Then she said she would take the deposit, but Anne would first have to fill out a form. She explained the purpose of the form and talked about money laundering and the bank's policy. Anne asked me what my plans were for the money. I told her I had just started working with a financial planner and this was one of the first steps in getting my plan on the road. I also told her that I was sure I would be back to see her after our next meeting."

"This is usually what happens at a bank when someone brings in a large deposit of cash, especially if it's not something the client does regularly."

"So," asked Peter, "what are the next steps?"

"Peter," I replied, "I'm a little concerned that your monthly expenses are only about a third of your total income, yet you've been working for four years and have savings of only $16,600. Can you tell me where all the money goes?"

"I didn't tell you that I give my parents $500 every time I receive my paycheque. They're saving this money for me — for when I'm ready to get married and purchase my first home."

"I expect these expenses are to be paid in cash?"

"Well, I don't know," said Peter.

"Another question is where is all this money being saved?"

"I'm not at liberty to say, but I know where this money is and so do my parents."

"I respect that, Peter, but by now you know how complex it is to convert your home savings 'account' to a legitimate a bank account. I recommend that you discuss with your parents the idea of putting your biweekly savings in the bank."

"That's a great idea," said Peter.

"Peter, I'm recommending that you go to your bank and make an appointment with Anne. I'll explain what you should discuss with her to enable you to get a credit card. You see, Peter, since your bank doesn't know how well you handle credit, I'm suggesting that you discuss getting a secured credit card."

"What do you mean by a secured credit card?" asked Peter.

"A secured credit card is for a person who wants to have a credit card but has no credit history to support the request. That person gives the credit card company $1,000, for example, and the company holds the $1,000 as security for the equal credit amount. In some cases the person might have to give 130 percent of the credit granted, which is done to cover interest charges that you may incur if you don't pay the credit back and the balance is sitting at the maximum plus interest."

"What does the bank do with the money I give them?" asked Peter.

"The money is usually held in a guaranteed investment certificate — a GIC — or a term certificate for a minimum of two to three years. It's in your name and earns interest during that period."

"Is the interest the same as I pay on the credit card?"

"Oh no," I said, trying to encourage him. "It's much lower than the price for getting the credit."

"It's all beginning to take shape," said Peter. "But when do I get my money back?"

"You get your money back after you have proven to the bank that you're capable of handling credit in a satisfactory manner and pay back the credit card as agreed. Or you might decide that you no longer need the credit card and you pay it off, in which case you request that the company close your card. Then the funds will be released to you."

"How much do you think is a reasonable request for a credit limit on a card?" asked Peter.

"I recommend that you ask for $1,000."

Peter replied, "That's exactly what I thought."

"Now, Peter, I have a few things I need you to do for our next meeting:

- Make an appointment with Anne at your bank. Tell her that you don't have a credit history but you would like to have one, and that you're prepared to put an equal amount of money on deposit for what the limit on the credit card will be. Let her know that you want a limit of $1,000 and that you're requesting the funds to be held in a term deposit for three years.
- Talk to your parents and discuss with them the idea that you would like to save your money in a bank account in your name, especially after the experience you had at the bank on your last visit with such a large deposit.
- Decide how much money you'll need for your miscellaneous expenses such as dinner, movies, lunch, hygiene, dry cleaning, and bus fare. We need to start planning for your financial future.
- Bring your last year's income tax assessment or notice of assessment. It's the document you receive from the government after you file your taxes."

"Why do we need that?" asked Peter.

"Do you remember when I told you a couple of weeks ago that I would discuss the benefits of a registered retirement savings plan with you? Well, we'll be discussing that at our next meeting."

Summary

- Keeping your savings at home or elsewhere can cause difficulty when converting them to a savings account with the bank. Large sums of money brought into the bank may cause suspicion about where the money came from.
- If you are saving up money at home, it is advisable to open an account under your name and put your savings there instead.

Tessa-Marie Shillingford

Reader's Notes

_____

_____

_____

_____

_____

_____

_____

_____

_____

_____

_____

_____

_____

_____

_____

_____

_____

Chapter 13

The Weekly Weigh-in

Angela and Lucas, Week Nine: Monitoring the Monster's Diet

"Doing the loan was very interesting. When we phoned Marva to make the appointment, she asked us to phone each of our credit card companies and get a payout figure to close the account. All the companies wanted to know why we were closing the cards. They even offered higher credit limits, but we decided we only wanted to close the accounts.

"Marva decided to give each of us a Visa card with a limit of $1,000 at an annual rate of 12.5 percent, with no annual fees."

"Well, that's a pretty good credit card, as cards go."

"Yes, we thought so too," said Lucas. "Marva had us sign letters asking the companies to close our accounts and telling them that payments were being made and for what amounts. This was all done while we were there. Before the payments were arranged she opened the joint account. Then she arranged for our payments and for the amounts coming from each of our accounts to go into the joint account."

"It looks like Marva is well-informed about her financial institution's products and services."

"Most certainly," said Angela. "She said we should talk to her about an RRSP and our non-registered savings, and she asked us whether we had given any thought to buying our own home. We told her that we would be working with you in all those areas, now that we have the loan in place. She said she looks forward to assisting us with whatever she can."

"Marva knows the value of great customer service. And she's benefited from the way you talk about her — I'd recommend my friends to her," said Angela.

"What I would like to see now is your financial plan for the next year. It should look entirely different from your first financial picture. Let's begin with Lucas's plan."

Lucas's Plan

Rent	$800.00 (no increase)
Car	490.00 (no increase)
Gas	275.00 (10% increase)
Credit cards	—
Hygiene	100.00
Clothing	200.00
Groceries	200.00
Golf membership	100.00
Gym	37.50 (family plan)
Pocket change	400.00
Cellphone	30.00 (new plan)
Cable	110.00
Car insurance	200.00
Loan payment	576.00
Magazines	20.00
Total	**$3,538.50**

Net pay biweekly: $2,008 × 26/12 = $4,350.66 per month
Monthly income less expenses: $4,350.66 - $3,538.50 = $812.16

"Lucas, this is quite different from what you discussed with me when you first came to see me."

"Yes, it is. I feel more on track and a lot more focused. Now I can see where this is going. I never realized before that I needed to control my spending habits. Now I'm looking at a plan for the future."

"Do you think you can follow this plan through?"

"I know I can. Angela and I discussed our plans, and what we want at the end of three years is that the loan will be paid and we'll be married and purchasing our own home. Our plans will probably need some changes as we go forward, but now we *have* a plan."

"Planning your finances is like planning a trip. It's very important that you know where you're going, how you plan to get there, and what you will do once you've arrived. This will prevent you from ending up someplace you don't want to be, and you'll be better prepared for detours. With your finances it's the same thing: What are your goals? When do you want to achieve those goals? How do you plan to get there? Do you have a contingency plan for detours?" I wanted them to get the message without lecturing them too much.

"Angela, now it's your turn. May I look at your financial plan?"

Angela's Plan

Car payment	$294.00
Gas	150.00 (10% increase)
Credit card	—
Hygiene	100.00
Food	200.00
Clothing	200.00
Gym membership	32.50
Magazines	20.00
Car insurance	60.00
Cellphone	30.00
House phone	50.00
P.C.	400.00
Loan payment	288.00
Total	**$1,824.50**

Net pay biweekly: $1550 × 26/12 = $3,258.33 per month

Monthly income less expenses: $3,358.33 − 1,824.50 = $1,533.83

"I decided to save $400 biweekly in a non-registered retirement plan and $307.92 in an RRSP to take advantage of my RRSP contribution room. Lucas and I decided that we can stay on this plan for the next three years. We can both take full advantage of using our RRSP contributions towards a home purchase along with the amount we have in our non-RRSP account. We should have approximately $80,000 combined."

"Angela, I'm very proud of the steps that both you and Lucas have made in your financial plans. I'll keep them with me for the week and take a close look at them. Then we'll discuss them at length at our next meeting. I hope you have copies at home?"

"Yes, we have several copies."

"Take another look at them and see if there are any changes you would like to make. Take care of yourself, and I'll see you in a week."

Summary

- Have a clear plan for your financial journey. Know where you are going, how you plan to get there, and what you will do once you have arrived.
- Having a plan will prevent you from ending up someplace else.
- Create manageable goals and have a timeline with the steps you need to take to get there.
- Always have a contingency plan in case you have to make a detour.

Homework: Making a financial plan is a way of getting where you want to go. If you are going on a trip you plan when you want to go, then you book your vacation, followed by choosing the airline, booking a ticket, and deciding what you are going to wear when you get there and what restaurants you are going to eat at. You do all of this very carefully, but something as important as your financial life may have much less care put into it. You need to know what you want, and when and how you plan to get it all. Write down your recent revised financial plan. When you have it written down, go back to it and revise it again until you have it the way you want it to be.

Reader's Notes

Your revised financial plan:

_____

_____

_____

_____

_____

_____

_____

_____

_____

_____

_____

_____

_____

_____

_____

_____

_____

Now re-revise your financial plan:

_____

_____

_____

_____

_____

_____

_____

_____

_____

_____

_____

_____

_____

_____

_____

_____

_____

_____

_____

Chapter 14

Peter's Road to Financial Independence

Peter, Week Four: A Clear Financial Road

"Hello," said Peter, with a big smile on his face. "Do you know that I've had an amazing week?"

"I'm happy to learn that," I said.

"You gave me specific things to work on and I started the very next day. So I'll begin with the bank. I phoned and made an appointment to see Anne. I explained to her what I needed to do and she immediately purchased a guaranteed investment certificate for me with a three-year term and restrained it. She explained that 'restrained' means it's held as collateral for my credit card. She then submitted my application for the credit card. Anne also discussed savings and registered retirement savings plans, but I told her I was working with you and that it was on your recommendation that I came see her. She said she would have an answer on my application for the credit card in a few minutes, it was accepted, and I'll be receiving my new card by registered mail in a week.

"My other task was not so easy. Speaking with my parents about depositing the money in a bank account instead of a cash box was quite difficult. I talked to them about it for the entire week. I explained that if something were to happen to them, I would have to go to the bank with all that cash in the box and it would be very time-consuming and awkward.

"At the end of the week my parents said they had discussed what I'd told them—and they had gone to see the bank manager, who told them he would make an exception and take all that cash. My father said the manager explained to them that money in the bank is protected by the Canada Deposit Insurance Corporation up to $100,000 per account holder, per account ownership. My parents said they felt relieved—and pleased—because keeping all that money at home had really weighed heavily on their minds."

"Peter, you did well, and so did your parents. I'm sure that it was your discussion with them that helped and encouraged them to take the proper steps with their savings."

"My other assignment was very easy. As you know, I save over 60 percent of my net income. My expenses are very small—I live with my parents and I don't pay rent or board. Here are my monthly expenses:

Peter's Expenses

Student loan	$360.00
Cellphone	60.00
Cable	131.00
Miscellaneous	500.00
Total	**$1,051.00**

"I spend $1,051 every month. So my monthly net income is $3,452."

"That's great. When you put things down on paper, you always get a sense of where things are going. I have a question for you, Peter. How did you arrive at $500 a month on miscellaneous expenses, and what are they?"

"I thought you would ask about that," said Peter. "I kept track of all my purchases for a week and I spent $110 that week. I also know that I wasn't restraining myself, so I think the amount is pretty accurate. Then I added $15 more and multiplied that by four."

"I have another question. Did you go out for dinner at all during the week?"

"No, I didn't, but I included $60 for dinners out, which is about what I spend when I do go out."

"Peter, you don't own a car, is that right?"

"Oh yes. I live right in the city, so I use public transportation."

"How much is that a week?"

"Oh, wait," exclaimed Peter. "I forgot that I buy a monthly pass for $100."

"We'll need to adjust your expenses to reflect the transit pass. It's very important, Peter, to write down your expenses to ensure you don't miss any. While I've provided you with some information to get you started, I recommend that you do a little more research on registered retirement savings. And I suggest that you visit the website for the Canada Revenue Agency. Its address is http://www.cra-arc.gc.ca."

Summary

- If, like Peter, you have no credit, speak to the bank about obtaining a secured credit card. For a secured credit card, you put an equal amount or a bit more (say, 130 percent) aside as collateral. This way the bank can issue a card to get your credit history going.
- Have the bank put the security for your credit card into a GIC (guaranteed investment certificate) or an account that will earn you interest for the next three years while you are establishing your credit.
- Money deposited into the bank is protected by the Canada Deposit Insurance Corporation (CDIC) up to $100,000 (Canadian) per account holder per account.

Reader's Notes

_____

_____

_____

_____

_____

_____

_____

_____

_____

_____

_____

_____

_____

_____

_____

_____

_____

_____

_____

_____

Chapter 15

Three Ways You Can Win with RRSPs

Peter, Week Five: A Sensible Savings Plan

"Peter, I told you that I would explain the benefit of a registered retirement savings plan, or RRSP. I believe now is the proper time. I realize that your primary interest is in finding a way to get credit and, most important, a credit card. You were able to do that with recommendations from me and we were also able to take care of a few areas of your financial plan."

"As I told you," said Peter, "I've turned a deaf ear to conversations about RRSPs because of my parents' views. So I have no idea about the benefits."

"An RRSP has three main benefits:
1. It allows Canadian taxpayers to save money for their retirement tax-free.
2. The government allows Canadians to use a maximum of $20,000 of their registered retirement savings towards the purchase of their first home.
3. The money can be used in your retirement years as income."

"I never knew how that worked. All I know is that my parents and their friends grumble every time they take money out of their RRSPs. They say that the government is charging income tax on their RRSPs and they should never have done that."

"As you know, Peter, I want you to take time to visit the Canada Revenue Agency website at http://www.cra-arc. gc.ca to gather as much information about RRSPs and their tax implications as you can.

"I do understand what your parents and their friends mean, and I'll explain it fully. Beginning with the tax-sheltered component, this is how it works. When Canadian taxpayers contributes to their RRSP, it is generally done through contributions that started when they begin to earn income from employment in Canada. These contributions can be made up to the age of 69. The years in between are usually your top earning years, so income earned during that period is taxed at a much higher rate—your tax bracket—than when you become a pensioner on a smaller fixed income, which would include a portion of the RRSP. By then you are not earning a salary, so you are taxed in a lower tax bracket. Even if you now have to pay income tax on that RRSP money, it is at a much lower rate than you would have paid at the time you earned it.

"You see, if you contribute $5,000 to an RRSP, when you prepare your tax return this amount is taken off your taxable income, which is listed on the T4 slip you receive from your employer. In your case, for example, if your taxable income is $75,000 and your employer remitted tax on your behalf to Revenue Canada based on that income, you have paid income tax on that amount. But with the RRSP contribution you now have $5,000 that you can subtract from your taxable income. So your new taxable income is now $70,000 instead of $75,000. When you purchase an RRSP, your financial institution sends you a tax receipt, which you enclose with your tax return to Revenue Canada. You will now receive a credit or a refund on the income tax your employer remitted on your behalf."

"It makes sense," said Peter. "I understand how that part works. I save all that money over those years without paying tax on it. Then when I begin to use it, I will pay tax but at a reduced rate."

"That's right," I said.

"But tell me about buying a home using my registered retirement savings," said Peter.

"Okay, this is how it works. You've purchased your first home, so you can now use up to $20,000 of your RRSP tax-free as part of your down payment. This withdrawal from your retirement savings plan is called the 'first-time home buyer's withdrawal.' When it is done by your financial institution, you don't create any tax implications."

"Can I use the money only towards my down payment?"

"No, it can also be used for moving expenses, legal fees, or anything to do with buying your new home at the time."

"Do I have to pay the money back?"

"Oh yes, you do."

"Is this a loan?"

"No, it isn't a loan. After you've been in your new home for two years, the government will send you a notice telling you that you need to pay back into your RRSP one-fifteenth of the amount you took from it."

"Why two years later, and why one-fifteenth of the total?" asked Peter.

"Well, the government gives you two years to organize your finances after making the single biggest purchase of your life. And the one-fifteenth means that you have fifteen years to pay it all back, free of interest. Remember how you subtracted the amount you contributed from your taxable income?"

"Yes."

"Now it's time to pay back. Instead of subtracting that year's full $5,000 payment from your taxable income, you would now subtract only $3,667. The other $1,333 would be the portion you need to pay back."

"That's amazing!" exclaimed Peter. "I still make only my regular contribution — I thought I needed to make a loan payment. I understand this better now. When I retire I will be able to withdraw from my registered retirement income. There are three ways for me to win as a taxpayer with an RRSP:

1. tax-free savings

2. money to help me buy a home

3. retirement income

"I like that. Now what do I do about opening a registered retirement savings plan?"

"Well, Peter, you have some homework for our next meeting. I need you to tell me the amount of money you have left after expenses and how much you're prepared to put into your retirement savings. According to your assessment you have room for $29,000. So, I'll see you next week."

Summary

- Three main benefits of RRSPs:
- 1.They allow Canadian taxpayers to save money tax-free for their retirement.
- 2.The government allows Canadians to use a maximum of $20,000 of their RRSP towards the purchase of their first home.
- 3.The money can be used in your retirement years as income.
- Visit the Canada Revenue Agency website, http://www.cra-arc.gc.ca, for more information about RRSPs.
- Visit your financial institution website for additional information.

Tessa-Marie Shillingford

Reader's Notes

Chapter 16

Peter's Road to Financial Success

Peter, Week Six: Peter's Financial Plan

"Hello," said Peter. "How are you?"

"I'm great," I said. "How did you do with your homework?"

"I did everything you asked me to do. When I have a goal and a way to achieve that goal, I stick to it like glue."

"I am very impressed," I said. "Now, Peter, let me see what you have for me." Peter gave me a sheet of paper titled "My Revised Plan."

Monthly Expenses

Student loan	$360.00
Cellphone	60.00
Cable	131.00
RRSP	1,000.00
Non-registered savings	951.00
Transportation	200.00
Dry cleaning	150.00

Lunches, dinners, movies	400.00
Hygiene, etc.	200.00
Total	**$3,452.00**

"I see that you've accounted for everything this time."

"Yes," said Peter, "the first six items are the most important to me. Items seven through nine, I can control. There is one thing that I wanted to ask you, though. Should I pay off my student loan?"

"Well, Peter, you get to write off the interest that you pay on your student loan, which is a benefit, and the interest is very low. I recommend that at this time you continue to pay off the student loan as you're presently doing. You will need to go to your bank and meet with your financial services representative to open an RRSP and a non-registered savings plan."

"I have done some homework, though, and I have a few questions for you about different types of savings. I want to be able to discuss my options with the bank."

"Fire away," I said.

"Well, I've heard about mutual funds. What are they?"

"Mutual funds are a 'basket' of stocks that are professionally managed for you."

"How do they work?"

"The mutual fund manager picks and chooses stock that he feels will meet the needs of his investors."

"Who can buy them?"

"Any Canadian."

"Where can they be bought?"

"Any bank or trust company whose employees are licensed to sell these investments."

"Can you lose your money?"

"Yes, you can. Mutual funds are not protected by the Canada Deposit Insurance Corporation. So if the companies whose funds you hold should become insolvent, you will lose your investment. All investments have some inherent risk, and some investments—such as mutual funds and stocks—have more risk."

"This is very complicated," said Peter.

"Yes, it is, and that's why the person you deal with at the bank will help you make choices based on your answers to some very specific questions. When you meet with you bank to open your RRSP and non-RRSP savings, they will ask you how long you intend to keep your money invested, how often you plan to contribute, and how much. These are just some of the questions you will be asked, and your answers will help your bank assess your level of risk tolerance. And they'll be thorough, so you should let them know that your appointment is for investment choices.

"Peter, while I've provided you with some information to get started, I recommend that you do a little more research on mutual funds. A good place to start is at your financial institution. Also, several Internet sites provide useful information about investing in mutual funds and their associated risks. The Mutual Fund Dealers Association is a very good place to start; their website address is http://www.mfda.ca. Another good source of information is the Investment Institute of Canada; look for Investor Education on their website at http://www.ific.ca."

"Is there anything else I should know?" asked Peter.

"Remember to make your contributions regularly—biweekly— on the day you get paid, and have it done automatically for a specific amount."

"You know," said Peter, "I'm excited. I feel ready to take control of my financial future."

"Okay, Peter, I'll see you next week to make sure you fully understand where you are and how you expect to meet your financial goals."

Summary

- Mutual funds are a "basket" of stocks that are professionally managed for you.
- A mutual fund manager picks and chooses stocks that he/she feels will meet the needs of his/her investors.
- Any Canadian can buy mutual funds from any bank or trust company whose employees are licensed to sell these investments.
- Mutual funds are not protected by the CDIC, so there is a risk that you can lose your money.
- Mutual Fund Dealers Association website: http://www.mfda.ca
- investor education website: http://www.ific.ca
- Remember, make your contributions regularly.

Reader's Notes

_____

_____

_____

_____

_____

_____

_____

_____

_____

_____

_____

_____

_____

_____

_____

_____

_____

_____

_____

Chapter 17

Exuberant Peter

Peter, Week Seven: Our Last Meeting

Peter arrived smiling. He was very excited.

"I have two things to tell you. First, I got my credit card by registered mail."

"Great," I said.

"Second, I have another case for you."

"A case?" I questioned.

"Yes," replied Peter. "My barber is self-employed. I was telling him how you've helped me and he asked me to find out if you were willing to help him. He said he would pay you. And, by the way, how much do I owe you?"

"Peter, you don't owe me anything. All I ask of you is to teach everyone you meet about credit awareness. What I have given to you, I hope you will give to another. By doing that you help me meet my goal of enlightening, educating, and encouraging everyone I meet to handle their finances successfully."

"Really, that's all I have to do? Well, I'm already on my way. I've been telling my cousins about what I've learned, and my cousin John is coming to the bank with me to start his financial plan."

"I'm really pleased that you're sharing your financial knowledge."

"What about my friend the barber?" asked Peter.

"I will help your friend," I said. "We'll talk about him at the end of our session today. Meanwhile, what happened at the bank when you had your investment meeting?"

"I was so pleased. Anne, my bank representative, was very good. She explained everything to me, and what helped me the most was that I understood everything. I answered a series of questions that she explained would help her to recommend the proper mix for my investment portfolio. She said that since I have a long investment time range — and if I stay invested for the long run — I will do significantly better than if I had invested over a short term."

"It sounds to me that Anne took the time to explain to you the risk and volatility of the market," I said.

"She did. When it came to my non-registered retirement savings, I told her that I'll need this money for a car in two years and perhaps a trip in one year, and that I was hoping to purchase my own home in the next seven to ten years. She then asked me to answer some questions, keeping my goals in mind. So, for my non-registered investments, she chose some money market and income funds."

"How did you feel, Peter, after meeting with Anne?"

"I felt great. I felt for the first time that I was on course and that I had a plan to meet my financial goals."

"Did you stick to the plan we made?"

"Yes, I did, and so far I'm very comfortable with it."

"When you first came to see me you were searching for a solution to your lack of credit, and that was all you were seeking. But because I asked some key questions, I was able to uncover some needs you didn't realize you had. These were brought to the front of your mind and now you have a map for reaching your financial goal. Tell me, Peter, how does that now make you feel?"

"Well, I said to you when I met you that Lucas thinks you're a financial angel. I've been trying to outdo Lucas, and I must say I feel for the first time that I'm financially knowledgeable."

"I'm very pleased, Peter, to hear that. Now tell me more about the barber."

"My barber's name is Cuthbert. I've been going to him for at least eight years. For our first meeting I had to change the day I usually get my hair cut, and I told him it was because I had to meet with a financial advisor. He became curious, and the next time I saw him I told him what you were doing for me."

"Tell me a little about Cuthbert."

"Well, he's twenty-six years old and he rents a chair at the barber shop. He gets paid in cash. That's all I really know."

"Did he say what his needs were?"

"All he said was that he could use the advice of someone like you."

"Well, Peter, you can let your friend know that I'll be able to see him. As a matter of fact, he can come on the same day as you. Here are a few of my cards. You may give them to anyone you think can use my help."

"Are you sure I am not to pay you?" asked Peter again.

"Yes, my reward is seeing the twinkle in your eyes and the bounce in your step. Just teach another person, Peter. One person is all I ask of you, and if you do that I will have met my goal. Peter, I would like us to meet in one year's time to go over your plan and make the necessary changes."

"Changes?" asked Peter.

"Yes, changes — like a raise in pay, a new job, planning to get married, buying a new car."

"I understand," said Peter. "I'll be in touch before year-end — I'll call just to keep in touch. Thanks."

"It's my pleasure."

Peter left, smiling as he bounced down the steps.

Summary

- Always have ready your financial map of where to go.
- Expect changes to happen and that these changes will affect your financial plan. Assess your financial goals once a year to incorporate the changes into the plan and adjust accordingly.

Reader's Notes

Chapter 18

The Self-Employed Trap

Cuthbert, Week One: Taking Care of Your Business

Peter's friend Cuthbert called me the next evening, just as I was returning from answering the door. A lovely new plant had arrived—it was from Peter, expressing his gratitude. I was smiling as I answered the phone. Cuthbert introduced himself and I made an appointment to meet with him the next evening.

Cuthbert arrived a little later for his first appointment than we had planned. He explained that he had been delayed because his last client was late. He seemed a little shy as I invited him to sit.

"Tell me about you," I said.

"I'm twenty-six and I've been a barber for nine years. I live with my mother."

"What would you like me to do for you?" I asked.

"I really don't know what to say," he said. "I have no idea what I need. All I know is that I don't have anything to show for nine years of working."

"Let's start at the beginning," I said. "Peter told me you rent a chair at your barber shop. How does that work?"

"For the first five years I worked at a shop and was paid minimum wage. Then I met someone who told me I could make at least twice what I was being paid if I worked for myself. He told me that a friend of his rented a chair at a barber shop and he paid the rent from the money his clients paid him. I did some research and found a shop where I could rent a chair. I've been doing it for four years and I've doubled my income, but I'm still not showing any growth in my savings. I make all this money and it just disappears."

"How much is all that money?" I asked.

"I take in at a very minimum $700 a week to a maximum in the summer of $1,200 to $1,300 a week. But it's the same whether I make $700 or $1,300 a week — it all goes."

"Do you have a bank account?"

"Yes, I do."

"What type of account is it?"

"It's a personal account."

"Do you have a business account?"

"No, I don't," said Cuthbert.

"What do you do with the cash you collect from the clients?"

"I pay bills, I pay for my car, I pay for my chair, I give my mom money sometimes, I buy materials — I spend it all."

"Cuthbert, you need some financial business planning. Our meeting tonight will be short, but you have two very important things to do. First, I want you to register your business with the provincial government, at the Ministry of Consumer and Corporate Affairs, as a sole proprietorship.

Second, I want you to take the papers they give you and go to your bank and make an appointment to open a business account.

"As soon as the account is open I want you to deposit all the money you receive during the day every evening on your way home. The purpose of doing your deposit every day is so that you will know at the end of one week exactly how much money you earned. It will also help your bank become aware of your business patterns. That's all for today.

"You'll need to return next week after you've registered your business as a sole proprietorship. That's the cheapest and easiest type of business registration. Sole means 'one,' and proprietorship means 'ownership' — one owner, and that's you. And you should have opened your business account by then. Do you have a business name?"

"Yes, it's called Great Cuts."

"Also, bring me a list of all your expenses, including even what you spend for a pack of gum. I want to see every penny that you spend. See you next week."

Cuthbert looked a little stunned, but I felt he would follow my directions.

Summary

If you decide to be self-employed, it is important to follow certain guidelines. Ensure that your business is registered and you open a business account at your financial institution.

Homework: Self-employment does not mean "I am my own bank." Being self-employed means being diligent in the occupation you have chosen. Do it well; be organized, focused, and meticulous; and make sure you use your financial institution to your benefit. Take full advantage of the facilities that are there for you. Talk to your bank—they will be happy to help you.

Reader's Notes

If you're in business for yourself, can you relate? What will you do next?

_____

_____

_____

_____

_____

_____

_____

_____

_____

_____

_____

_____

_____

_____

_____

_____

_____

Chapter 19

My Pocket Is My Bank

Cuthbert, Week Two: Keeping Track of Your Transactions

"Good evening," said Cuthbert, still appearing a little shy.

"Hello, how was your week?"

"I really enjoyed my week. After I left you, I spoke to Peter and discussed what you'd asked me to do. Peter helped me register my business online. We came across one snag, though: there was another business with the same name. So we changed the name to Great Cuts by Cuthbert, and that worked. Then Peter made me an appointment to meet with a lady named Marjory at his bank, and she opened my business account."

"How did that go?"

"She explained how the account works. She also asked me how many transactions I would have each month, including deposits, and how much money I would be depositing at a time. I told her that since I was dealing in cash, you suggested that my deposit should be daily, and I told her I work six days a week. She further explained that business accounts are charged for deposits and withdrawals. She told me her bank has different service plans based on the number of transactions, and recommended that to start I take a service plan in the middle range. Then she said that, since I was a referral from Peter, she would waive my service fees for three months. During those three months she would be able to get a better idea of my business banking needs."

"Marjory seems to be a very knowledgeable lady."

"Yes, she is, and she also listens. She keeps her eyes on you and you can see that she really wants to make your banking experience comfortable and relaxed. Marjory gave me a deposit card and suggested that I use the automated banking machine to avoid the long lines for the tellers. Then she asked my permission to do a credit check. She explained that she was doing this to see if I qualified for any of her bank's credit products.

"Unfortunately, I didn't, because when I went to college I received a $500 credit card and didn't pay my bill. I did finally pay the bank back, but only after the bill went through a collection agency. Marjory explained that it would take seven years before my credit rating would improve, so there are a few restrictions on my account."

"Cuthbert, that's how financial institutions work. You're not the first young man I've met who's in the same situation. Throughout our meetings we'll explore this further and see what we can do to improve your credit. Did you complete the list of expenses for me?"

"Yes, here it is."

Cuthbert's Monthly Expenses

Car payment	$458
Insurance	320
Supplies	250
Chair rental	350
Gas	200
Total	**$1,578**

"Is that it, Cuthbert?"

"Yes."

"But you make at least $2,000 to $4,800 a month. Where does the rest go?"

"I spend it, I guess."

"But you can't guess," I said. "You must know, Cuthbert. Okay, let's do this together. I'm going to break it down.

"We know there are five things you spend your money on, but we also know there is a lot not accounted for. Let's both put our heads together and look for it. Do you pay for living with your mom?"

"If she needs money, she asks me," Cuthbert said offhandedly.

"How much is that?" I asked.

"Three to four hundred dollars"

"Okay, do you buy clothes?"

"Yes," he said, smiling.

"How much do you spend on that?"

Cuthbert answered confidently, "Three hundred and fifty dollars."

"How often do you spend that much?"

"I don't know," he said.

"Do you have a girlfriend?"

"Yes."

"Do you go out to dinner with her?"

"Yes."

We were getting somewhere.

"Who pays?"

"Sometimes she does. It costs about $150."

"How often do you two go out?"

"About twice a month."

"What about movies?"

"That's included."

"Cuthbert, how much money do you have in your pocket right now?"

"That's easy," he said. "Nothing."

"Nothing," I repeated.

"Yes, I deposited everything I made this past week, and I didn't know if I should take any money out. I asked Peter and he suggested I discuss that with you."

He was serious. I couldn't help but smile.

"I'm very sorry, Cuthbert," I said. "I didn't mean you should be walking about with empty pockets."

"That's okay," said Cuthbert. "I had $100 when I last saw you and it wasn't my turn to pay for dinner. My mom didn't ask me for money, so I just thought I would wait to discuss it with you as Peter suggested."

"Tonight we'll put some plans in place to help you avoid this situation."

Cuthbert's Revised Monthly Expenses

Car payment	$458
Insurance	320
Supplies	250
Chair rental	350
Gas	200
Mom	350
Clothes	200
Dinners/movies	200
Total	**$2,328**

"Cuthbert, do you most often make $700 or $1,200?"

"I make more like $1,100 a week. It is very unusual to make just $700 a week. It usually happens when I work only five days, in January or February."

"In this case let's use an average income of $1,000 weekly. What about income tax?"

"What do you mean?" asked Cuthbert.

"I mean, have you filed income tax returns?"

"No," said Cuthbert.

"Well, this is April," I said, "Are you going to file your tax return?"

"Well," said Cuthbert, "I didn't think I had to."

"Did you work last year?"

"Yes, I did."

"Do you have copies of all of your expenses — receipts for rent and other purchases for your business?"

"Yes, I do"

"What about the amounts your clients paid?"

"Yes, I have records of that."

"Well, you're all set to see an accountant. Cuthbert, you should go to an accountant or a tax preparation company to prepare your income tax return. You'll find these firms in your local newspaper. The purpose of completing an income tax return is to let the government know that you are employed. If you don't file an income tax return, the government will assess you anyway and then you'll have to pay taxes *and* penalties. It's not a nice experience. You'll also be able to open a registered retirement plan and take advantage of its tax sheltering for some of your income.

"As a self-employed taxpayer you will also have to submit your Canada Pension Plan contribution. Cuthbert, I would also like to make a recommendation to you about your business account. Make an appointment to see Marjory at the bank and ask her to open a business savings account. The purpose is to set aside 20 percent of your earnings to cover taxes and contributions to your Canada Pension Plan. Also, ask her to explain RRSP and non-RRSP savings. And I recommend that you do a little more research about running a small business. The government's Internet site will give you the information you need to make educated decisions. The address of the Canada Revenue Agency website is http://www.cra-arc.gc.ca.

"And your expenses will have to be adjusted one last time."

"This financial planning seems really complicated."

"Yes, it is," I said, "But if the plan is followed, it can be very rewarding."

Cuthbert's Final Monthly Expenses

Car payment	$458
Car insurance	320
Supplies	300
Chair rental	350
Gas	200
Mom	350
Clothes	200
Dinner/movies	200
20% of gross income	400
RRSP	200
Non-RRSP	450
Bank charges	72
Balance in business account	500
Total	$4,000

"Cuthbert, this finally balances to your average income for one month of $1,000 a week."

"This looks great," said Cuthbert. "I don't understand what I did with my money. I never had savings."

"This financial plan may still not work, Cuthbert. The only way to be sure it works is to be disciplined with your deposits and to arrange for all the transfers to be done on a specific date every week. I am also recommending that you pay yourself with a cheque every week and then make the transfer to your personal RRSP and savings."

"What about my mom? I would prefer to have it deposited in her account automatically. When I offer her money she often doesn't take it, and then two weeks later she might ask for money and of course I'm short at the time. I would prefer to have it done regularly."

"Cuthbert, talk to your mom and ask her how much she needs. Then make sure you give her that amount every week."

"That's a great idea. I'll explain to her why and I know she'll go along with it, especially if I let her know that it's your recommendation."

"I also recommend that you meet with an accountant who specializes in small business. He or she will recommend the best way to pay yourself and the taxes, and the benefits to you. What we've done just gets you started. We'll make further changes."

"That's really good. I'm excited, and looking forward to getting my business in order."

"We've covered a great deal this evening. I'll see you next week, same time. One more thing—make sure to ask Marjory about a secured Visa card to help you establish your credit again."

Summary

- Make sure your financial institution is telling you everything that you need to know.
- If your credit rating is not that great, do not feel that you're the only person in that situation. Take responsibility for your actions and keep in mind that it could take up to seven years before your credit rating improves.

- For small business owners, make sure to set aside some time to see an accountant to help prepare your income tax return.
- It is highly recommended to set aside 20 percent of small business earnings to cover taxes and contributions to your Canada Pension Plan (CPP).
- Canada Revenue Agency website: http://www.cra-arc.gc.ca

Reader's Notes

Chapter 20

"Things Are Now in Order"

Cuthbert, Week Three: Taking Charge of Your Business

"Hello, Cuthbert. How are you this evening?"

"I feel great—I'm now well on my way to taking charge of my finances. I'm so pleased that you showed me how. I met with an accountant, and we'll be meeting again next week with all my papers. And he'll be preparing my income tax. His fee to prepare everything is $250. He said that, if I'm satisfied with him, we should meet on a monthly basis to keep my records and taxes up-to-date."

"Well, Cuthbert, I'm happy you've taken those steps towards preparing your income tax."

"I also spoke to my mother and we decided that I'll give her that same amount of money every Friday. She feels much better about that plan, and I think she's much happier now that she won't have to ask me for money when she needs it.

"Marjory at the bank wasn't able to help me with the credit card at this time. She suggested that I build my savings and create a history of managing my account as agreed, and then she will apply for the credit card. I feel comfortable working with Marjory, so I'll follow her advice. I now have a registered savings and a non-registered savings account. My contributions to my registered accounts will begin after I receive my income tax return."

"Cuthbert, you've successfully prepared yourself for a great future. All your plans to help you attain your goals are now in place. I recommend that you follow this plan for a year. Unless you have major changes things should stay the same. If something suddenly turns up, you should get in touch with me to revise your financial plan.

"This is our last meeting. If the plan turns out to be too rigid or if you want to make changes, remember, you can give me a call and I'll be happy to help implement the changes.

"Cuthbert, I'm giving you a few of my business cards. Please feel free to pass them on to your friends or family."

"I am happy you said that. I intended to ask your permission to recommend you to my friends and family. Thank you for all your help." Cuthbert looked happy.

"Well, Cuthbert, have fun successfully handling your finances." I shook his hand and sent him off.

Summary

- Taking charge of your finances is just one step to success.
- Follow the plan to help attain your goals for a year. Unless there are major changes, things should remain the same.
- If something does turn up, look at revising your financial plan.

Tessa-Marie Shillingford

Reader's Notes

Chapter 21

The Monster's Maintenance Diet

Lucas and Angela, Week Ten: Maintaining Your Plan

"Hello Angela, Lucas. This is our last meeting, so we going to discuss the Debt Monster's maintenance diet. I took a good look at your revised plans, and they're great. I recommend that you follow them for one year. What do you think? Did you make any other changes?"

"No, we didn't," said Lucas. "We spent a few hours going over the plans and then decided we're happy with them. We want to follow them as they are for a year, as you recommended, unless you came up with changes."

"No, I didn't, but I wanted to let you know I think it's quite a drastic change from what you did before meeting with me."

"Yes, it is, but we plan to try it anyway. We know that if we don't work on it we won't be able to meet our three-year goal."

"I'm pleased with your determination, and I'm confident that you'll both stay focused and work on the plan together.

If any big changes take place, like a promotion or any other changes, please remember that I'll be happy to help you with the revisions."

"Great," said Angela. "We definitely want to follow this plan—we're very anxious to keep the Monster on this maintenance diet. We're so much more relaxed. Since we made these financial changes we feel that we've really taken charge of our financial future."

"This is a far cry from our first meeting."

"Yes," said Lucas, "and we're really pleased that we made those changes with your guidance. May I have a few of your business cards? I've recommended you to some of my co-workers and they would like to come to see you. Are you going to start charging for your services?"

"No, my mission is to help."

"We've already taken so much of your time," said Lucas, "so we won't take any more of it this evening. Once again, thank you so very much. You are a wonderful person."

"See you soon on a social level. And have a wonderfully charged week." I gave them both a big hug. As they were about to leave, I added, "Lucas and Angela, while I've provided you with some information to get started, I recommend that you do a little more research on registered retirement savings and the First-time Home Buyers Program. The government's Internet site will give you all the information you need to make educated decisions. The Canada Revenue Agency's website is http://www.cra-arc.gc.ca."

Summary

Make sure you keep the Debt Monster on its diet plan.

Homework: Write down how you will keep the Monster on its diet.

Reader's Notes

Your Monster's diet plan:

_____

_____

_____

_____

_____

_____

_____

_____

_____

_____

_____

_____

_____

_____

_____

_____

_____

How do you plan to keep the Monster on its diet?

_____

_____

_____

_____

_____

_____

_____

_____

_____

_____

_____

_____

_____

_____

_____

_____

_____

_____

_____

Chapter 22

The Emergency Stop

The phone was ringing. It sounded loud and impatient, as if it knew it was an emergency.

"Hello?" I answered. A rush of jumbled up words poured into my ears; I caught only the word "Aunt." Then I said, "Whichever one of you it is, please talk more slowly — and calm down. Who am I speaking to?"

"Angela," the voice said.

"Hello, Angela. I didn't recognize your voice. What is going on?"

The rush of words started again. "Slow down," I said. "I can't understand one word you're saying."

She repeated, "Lucas and I went on a vacation. Now the car isn't working, and we haven't been able to rest. Can we come over now?"

"No," I said. "I'm helping someone at the moment. What about tomorrow evening, as this requires a little more information from you. Maybe you can help me understand what your vacation and your car not working is all about."

I heard a big sigh. "Well, that's okay, but just so you know, it's a mess," replied Angela.

"Thanks for the warning," I said. "I'll see both of you tomorrow evening at 7 p.m."

The next evening, Angela and Lucas walked in looking very troubled.

"What's going on?" I asked.

"Well, it started with our friends calling to say that they had found this amazing vacation offer that they couldn't pass up. They thought that Lucas and I could get in on it and go with them on this vacation. Well, we did go. We've been back just three weeks and now our car has broken down."

"What about using your emergency funds for the car repairs?" I inquired.

Another big sigh. "That's the problem. You see, when we were invited to go on the holiday we had just enough money in the vacation account for one ticket. So, since we really wanted to go, we decided that we could take the funds from the emergency account to pay for the other ticket."

I nodded and made encouraging noises.

Angela continued, "The cost of the repairs is about $2,800 and we are short exactly $1,250. I really need the car to get to work. What can we do? As you know, we used all of the emergency fund *and* our vacation fund."

"Let's look at what got you into this predicament. Without looking at the plan you had in place, you made an impulsive decision to go on a trip you were not prepared for at all. You got caught up in your friends' excitement and allowed yourselves to make a decision that is having an impact on you now, three weeks later. And it will affect your cash flow for approximately a year or more.

"This is a very good lesson to have learned. Right now it's costly to you more in time than in money, but having this experience early in your life together will make such an impact on you that I'm sure nothing like this will happen again.

"My recommendation to you is to pay for the car repairs on your credit card, then use the money you've allocated from each paycheque for your emergency and vacation funds to pay off the credit card.

"We're really concerned about the Debt Monster moving in again," said Lucas.

"Stay on your plan and keep your eye on your goal. Don't get caught up in other people's plans. Always remember that the decisions you make today determines the life you live tomorrow. Now is the time for me to introduce the Circles to you, because I don't want to see you two get caught up in the unending cycle of debt. That's what the Debt Monster feeds on."

"What do you mean, Aunt Tess? What circles? We just wanted to take a vacation to reward ourselves for all our hard work!" exclaimed Lucas, sounding confused and frustrated.

"I know first-hand how hard you and Angela have been working the last few months," I said sympathetically. "But, as I said, you have to keep your eyes on your goal. When you decide to use your savings for unplanned expenses like vacations instead of what they were intended for, you're opening the door for the Debt Monster to walk back into your lives."

Angela and Lucas looked at me wide-eyed, eagerly waiting for my next words.

"When an emergency happens and you have no savings, you have no option but to turn to credit. This leaves you with bills at the end of the month that you didn't plan for. Because you haven't allocated for this end-of-the-month debt, you're short of cash to pay your bills. So you use the money you allocated for something else, like food, to pay your bills. But you still need money for food! So where do you turn?"

"To credit!" They answered in unison, their eyes still wide. I knew that they had just realized their mistake.

"Yes, credit," I answered, "and the Debt Monster. You both have two circles in your financial life, the circle of debt and the circle of savings. Right now your circle of debt is quite large: it's made up of your credit card payments, your student loans, and your car payments. You're both working actively to make this circle smaller, right?" I spoke firmly — it was time for the two of them to refocus.

"Right!" they declared together, with conviction.

"You also have your circle of savings. This circle is very small right now, but with determination and discipline, one day it will be bigger than the debt circle, right?"

"Right!" they again said together, even more confidently.

"Wrong!" I said, just as strongly. "Not if you keep giving in to temptation!" The confidence drained out of Angela's face and Lucas turned his eyes to the floor. "When you are faced with an emergency, which circle do you turn to — debt or savings?"

"Savings," answered Angela quietly.

"Right," I responded. "Your savings circle may get smaller, but opening your debt circle to pay for the emergency is much more dangerous. When you open your debt circle for emergencies, you are also opening it to high interest rates and monthly payments. The debt circle grows *four times* as fast as the savings circle. A small mistake in judgment can affect your financial plan for a full year, if not longer."

"But what if our savings circle isn't big enough to cover the emergency?" Lucas asked.

"Well, you use what savings you do have, and take only what you absolutely have to from your credit. You then have to continue saving while actively working to pay off your emergency debt. That way your savings circle will continue to grow. Your debt circle will get a little bigger, but not as big as it would have been if you had paid for the emergency completely from credit. And because you will be actively paying off the debt, the debt circle will keep getting smaller. By doing this, your savings circle will always be growing and available for emergencies.

"The whole idea of having a financial plan is to stay on the plan. It's like going on a trip—you may have to take a detour along the way, but you always keep your destination in mind. If you don't have a map of where you want to go, you will certainly get lost. This is exactly what happened to you both when you decided to go on that vacation you weren't prepared for. You both got lost, and now it's costing you time and money, just as it would if you were lost on a trip."

"Wow," said Lucas, "we really got off track, didn't we? I guess we must look pretty foolish to you."

"Nonsense," I exclaimed, giving them both a hug. "You've learned an important lesson. I'm sorry it had to be learned the hard way, but I'm sure that from now on you'll be travelling the straight and narrow path!"

Summary

- Sometimes we act impulsively and, without consulting our plans, we make decisions that can impact our lives even weeks after the decision was made.
- Some of our decisions could affect cash flow for a year or more.
- When you have decided to dip into that emergency fund and then realize that you need the money for something else, you may have to sacrifice some of the money allocated from each paycheque for your emergency or vacation fund to pay off the credit cards.
- Remember, the decisions you make today determines the life you live tomorrow.
- There are two circles in our financial life: the circle of debt and the circle of savings.
- In the case of an emergency, it is best to turn to the circle of savings before the circle of debts. The savings circle may get smaller, but it is more dangerous to use the circle of debt.

Reader's Notes

Write down your plan for emergencies:

_____

_____

_____

_____

_____

_____

_____

_____

_____

_____

_____

_____

_____

_____

_____

_____

_____

_____

_____

_____

_____

Chapter 23

Dreams Can Come True

Being Disciplined Pays Off

Angela and Lucas continued with their financial plan for the next three years, making only small adjustments when they received raises. Once they each had $20,000 in their RRSP, they decreased the portion going to the RRSPs and transferred a greater amount to non-registered savings. They planned to use the $40,000 towards the purchase of a home, while the larger portion in the non-registered savings would pay the balance of the 25 percent down payment and closing costs, which include lawyer's fees, government fees, and moving costs.

They have now both withdrawn the money from their RRSPs to use towards the down payment on their new home, which will be ready in nine months. The purchase price was $275,000 and 25 percent of that is $68,750. The closing date is September 15.

The best news is that I will be attending their wedding in July. The cost of the wedding is being taken from their savings, which will now decrease because they'll have a mortgage to pay. They are concentrating on establishing an emergency fund equal to six months of their living expenses. When this is in place, they will begin saving for their annual vacation and their future plan of starting a family.

Since we last met, Peter purchased a car and became engaged to the young lady he met through Lucas and Angela. He is saving for getting married one day and purchasing a home. Cuthbert continued with his financial plan and is now a solid taxpayer, taking advantage of the privilege of tax-sheltered savings. He is saving so that one day he will be able to run his own shop, where he will be the one renting out chairs to other barbers. Cuthbert and his girlfriend are planning to get married in three years and buy their own home.

My message to every person who reads this book is to realize that a little planning—and lots of focus and discipline—will enable anyone to have a great financial future. Making sure that you pay automatically into savings, both registered and non-registered, is the best thing you can do for yourself. My wish and hope is that I have been able to enlighten, educate, and encourage you to handle your finances successfully.

Thank you for giving me the opportunity to open your financial mind.

Summary

A little planning, focus, and discipline will enable anyone to have a great financial future.

Reader's Notes

How are you doing?

_____

_____

_____

_____

_____

_____

_____

_____

_____

_____

_____

_____

_____

_____

_____

_____

_____

_____

_____

Testimonials

The practical advice and simple step-by-step financial plan she gave me saved my sanity, dissolved my stress and let me enjoy my life again! She said, "Don't tell me what you don't want, tell me what you want." And then she showed me how to get it. I only wish I'd met her 20 years ago. Jan Shepherd

Hi Tessa,

Thank you for sorting out my financial mess and teaching me how to plan.

With Gratitude

Jackie C

Jan 17th 2009

Dear Tessa,

Thank you for your warmth, honesty & professionalism during our 1st meeting. I do appreciate your steadfast efforts to start me on the right track towards obtaining financial freedom. I'm aware that there is lots of work on my part that must be done and I'm ready. God has placed you in my life for a reason. I am a little tree, ready to be watered ..... to grow & be fruitful under your guidance.

Thanks for all your efforts in advance

Sharon

To Tessa,
My Mentor.

Thank you for all your support & encouragement with words so wise, you've motivated me, and showed me how to start & finish. To skillfully gain. and respect my earnings

Because of this, I'm now in my own home

You are always on hand for advice, continuing to show me ways of achieving my goal

Could not have done it without you

All this I offer with heartful THANKS

Florisca (F/o) Greenic

158

"Tessa"

This is a note of thanks to you, for handling my Finances in such a Proffesional & Effecient way.

You are an incredible lady & much to be credited. I will pay there is none like you absolutely none.

I am now finding it things much easier & definetely I will recommend you to Others. Sincerely Beryl Wrig

Tessa-Marie,

Thank you so much for helping me with everything.

You are inspiring and I really found the book helpful.

Take your knowledge and continue to share it with the world.

Richelle

Tessa & Brian,

Merry Christmas! Wow a lot has happened in a year and we couldn't have done it without you! This winter we are both going to hit the ski hills for the first time! When in Rome right? We've had a few bumps in the road but the lessons really have made it worth it. We're going on a real vacation in the new year some where warm and where the sun shiny for me then 6 hrs a day. Thanks for keeping an eye on #34, god knows it's a big job! We wish you all the best for the new year. Eat lots, Drink lots and enjoy everyone!

Merry Christmas)
Love
Kathleen
+
Sean

Kathleen's Story

Well we have crossed the one year mark, I can't believe how fast it went by! Life is good, I have met more people and have been going out socially which I have really enjoyed. The new job has been great. I'm working for the government in Foster Care and still working part time at the GAP. Sean still liking his job and has become the senior installer for Edmonton. He got to travel a couple of times this year for work and enjoyed the change. We had a lot of visitors come in August and September which was wonderful!! Mom and Dad were here as well as couple of friends. Kate came later in September and Sean had some guys here in October.

With all the fun and excitement of everyone coming, we got a little off track with our spending. Visa's were used, excuses were made, through it was a fabulous time we both literally woke up one day in October and realized what a mess we had made. All I kept saying to Sean was "Tessa would kill us!" We made a quick re-payment plan, hit a couple more bumps in the road but we have made it through. We had to say no to dinners with friends, bought groceries only when they were on sale (you can imagine the creative meals we had!) On Friday we made the last payment that we will ever make to a credit card again. We cut 3 up (we have the pieces in a baggie) and put last one in a bag of water and put it in the freezer, so if we ever think we absolutely need it, we'll have to wait at least 48 hours for it to melt.

We were attacked by the Greed monster that showed us a great time but later called out his big brother the Debt monster to party with us. The party was so good that brothers called there sister the Regret monster and her twin sisters Disappointment and Anger. Sean and I decided that they only way to not get invited to this party again was to make sure it was a lesson for the both of us. Life was crappy, I cried, Sean sulked. I worked more shifts to try to get it paid back faster, so when I wasn't working I was sleeping. On Friday when we made the last payment, it made it all worth it!!!! All of our money is ours! (well except the bit we owe to the line of credit which GAP hours are going to pay off in a couple of months)

So now I'm emailing you to ask you to TAKE OUR MONEY!! We have got another $10,000 in the house account. Which makes a total for the first year of $21, 000 towards our house! Our goal for this year is to pay off the Line of Credit, take an real vacation somewhere hot, not use a credit card and have $30 000 in the house account. What do you think??

Have a Good one !
   Kathleen

Thanks

To my husband, Bryan, and children, Gillian, Vanessa, and Michael, who supported me during the writing of this book.

I would like to say a special thanks to some very important people who helped me in putting this book together. To Carlotta and Duncan Winston, who inspired me while working with them at the start of their financial journey; to Florisca and James Gregoire for helping me to realize the need for this book; to O'Neil Campbell, my barber, who was so anxious to learn how to be a real businessman.

Special thanks to Carlotta, Laura, Janette, Jay and Joe and Wendy-Anne for helping me with typing and encouraging me to complete this book, and to my editor, Gillian Watts, for helping me get my message across.

About the Author

Tessa-Marie Shillingford was born in Dominica, West Indies, and immigrated to Canada in 1967. She spent a number of years working in government services, first with the West Indies Trade Council and then the Ontario Ministry of Education. Being a successful and savvy businesswoman, in 1980 she established and managed her own business teaching ceramic arts.

With her unique business experience and ability to communicate effectively, Tessa-Marie has been a guest speaker for numerous groups and associations, where she enlightens her audience on the benefits of proper financial management.

Currently Tessa-Marie Shillingford is a manager of financial services for a leading financial institution. She is a designated Personal Financial Planner, including personal financial counselling, by the Institute of Canadian Bankers, and is thus eminently qualified to provide her exceptional insight into personal financial and credit management.

Tessa-Marie resides in Toronto, Ontario, with her husband, Bryan, and has three children, Gillian, Vanessa, and Michael.

Printed in the United States
214337BV00003B/1/P